Starting the Colt

by MARY TWELVEPONIES

artwork by
BARBARA LOPEZ

THE
STEPHEN GREENE PRESS
PELHAM BOOKS

THE STEPHEN GREENE PRESS/PELHAM BOOKS

Published by the Penguin Group
Viking Penguin, a division of Penguin Books USA Inc., 375 Hudson Street,
  New York, New York 10014, U.S.A.
Penguin Books Ltd., 27 Wrights Lane, London W8 5TZ, England
Penguin Books Australia Ltd., Ringwood, Victoria Australia
Penguin Books Canada Ltd., 2801 John Street, Markham, Ontario, Canada L3R 1B4
Penguin Books (N.Z.) Ltd., 182-190 Wairau Road, Auckland 10, New Zealand

Penguin Books Ltd., Registered Offices: Harmondsworth, Middlesex, England

First published in 1990 by The Stephen Greene Press/Pelham Books
Distributed by Viking Penguin, a division of Penguin Books USA Inc.

10 9 8 7 6 5 4 3 2 1

Copyright © Mary Cleveland, 1990
All rights reserved
Illustrations by Barbara Lopez

Library of Congress Cataloging-in-Publication Data
Twelveponies, Mary.
  Starting the colt: the first two years of your horse's life / by
Mary Twelveponies ; art work by Barbara Lopez.
    p.   cm.
  ISBN 0-8289-0764-1: $16.95
  1. Horses—Training. 2. Western riding. 3. Driving of horse
-drawn vehicles. I. Title.
SF287.T976 1990
636.1'088—dc20   89-29879
                                      CIP

Printed in the United States of America
Set in Gill Sans and Primer Roman by Compset, Inc.
Designed by Deborah Schneider
Produced by Unicorn Production Services, Inc.

Contents

I
Method without Madness

In my books *Everyday Training: Backyard Dressage* and *There Are No Problem Horses— Only Problem Riders* I have given you instruction in training the horse and in curing his problems. Neither one fully explains how to get the colt started under saddle and safely through his first few rides so he is ready for training. I propose to do that here.

I have seen many articles describing a colt's first few lessons. It's true I haven't seen them all, but I have not been favorably impressed with what I have seen. Years ago one magazine had a cover picture of a horse with the question, "Will this horse be easy to break?" The colt had a very nice head with large, soft eyes expressing a tendency toward amenability. The article inside told the sad story. In essence, the colt was attacked by men with ropes who, without so much as a how do you do, awkwardly tried to restrain him as quickly as possible. The colt was frightened and proved the spirit his head indicated by fighting back. Of course he was hard to break under those circumstances. I often use ropes myself, but I do it with compassion and understanding and expertise.

There are a few who one day say, "Let's go ride the colt and see what he'll do." This is equivalent to asking a child on his first day in arithmetic class to work all the problems in chapter 20. Some people luck out doing this with the colt, but most of them end up with one or more problems to overcome. Regardless, it isn't fair to the colt. It's just acting out the romantic, but false, idea of how the West was won.

Red Cloud was a product of such thinking. In the first few weeks that Bill owned him, it seemed that everyone who came along claimed to have "broke that horse." We know for sure that two men and a woman had tried. Each of the two men said the horse was somewhat of an outlaw. He mistrusted women but had taken an instant liking for Bill, so Bill had no trouble riding him except for his occasional explosive bucking. If the first person who "broke" Red Cloud had educated him instead of just getting on and trying to ride out the storm, no one else would have had cause to make the same claim.

Today most people realize the colt should be given some sort of education before that first ride. Many recommend ground-driving or longeing. Either one or both are good—if they are done properly. If they teach the colt almost nothing or the wrong things, they are of no value or are actually detrimental.

There is a large group who drives a colt to a cart before riding him. It is true that this can teach him go, turn, and stop while he is still a little too young to be ridden, but it also has its drawbacks. The feel on the reins and the way the horse must accept them in driving is not exactly what you want when riding him. No matter how gentle a colt is or how controlled the driving environment, accidents can happen. An accident involving a cart is far harder to control and more likely to cause injury to the horse and/or the driver.

One must also bear in mind that it is just as foolish to hook him up without basic preparation as it is to just get on and ride him. And a colt can be too young to pull a cart, so you still don't gain that much time in teaching him the few basics he can learn in being driven.

Some will argue that driving is a way to develop his way of going as well as obedience. A youngster should be asked *only* for energetic, relaxed normal gaits whether driven or ridden, and he should not be cantered in the cart. I certainly don't condemn driving a colt. I just feel the disadvantages of driving outweigh the advantages for a great many of us.

I will just briefly mention training hitches. They can be useful under some circumstances. I have used two varieties myself. From experience I have found them of little value, even cruel, if you don't have a very good understanding of horses and the limitations of the hitches. As my experience grew, I found easier, more effective ways of achieving the few goals for which training hitches are recommended. I won't discuss them further.

There is one specific method of starting colts that I would like to mention here in some detail. That is Ray Hunt's formula. Ray is well known throughout the West for his unique approach. I have watched him several times working with colts and their riders at his clinics. Several articles have been written praising his way with horses.

Briefly, this is his method. He goes into the round corral with the loose colt. Through the use of his body language and the lass rope he carries, he moves the colt around the corral, reverses him both inward and outward, and stops him, repeating the performance several times. When the colt will stand for his rubbing and patting him over his body, Ray puts the saddle on him and puts him through his paces again. Then the colt is turned loose in the arena. The colt isn't haltered, bridled, or restrained with the rope around his neck at any time.

2

Stopping a corralled colt with body language. The hand and rope flung out represent to him another horse cutting him off.

The following day the colts are brought into the round corral and the riders saddle them. They then mount and are all turned out into the arena, still without anything on the colts' heads. Ray mounts his horse and herds them back and forth, getting the horses to move out freely in all gaits. Miraculously, few riders have been hurt.

Ray is a master horseman. He understands the horse's body language and knows how to position himself, wave his hand, or toss his rope to get the colt to respond the way he wants. I don't know whether or not he rides a colt the first few times without bridle or halter himself. I think his reason for having the pupils do it is so they won't be pulling on the reins and discouraging the colts in moving out.

I have seen other good horsemen try to use this method and fail. I had a firsthand account from the owner of a gentle, willing Arabian colt about a professional trainer who was obviously trying to use it. Even though he may have been successful with all the others he had handled, he failed miserably with this one, scaring the colt out of his wits until he was practically a basket case. The trainer kept repeating Ray's philosophy to the owner, "I have to get his mind," and adding, "he just won't give it to me and I can't go on until he does." He had been at this well over a month and should have known to change his approach practically at the outset.

Method without Madness

I am a good horseman. I understand the horse's body language and can use my own to influence him. I just wouldn't use this method because it leaves out so much and can actually be much harder work than my own, more conventional, method. I can't recommend Ray's method to anyone because it requires a very special understanding and delicate touch that very few have. It also requires a lot of trial and error before a person could become consistently successful. It's fun to watch, though!

I've gone through a lot of trial and error and learning over the years. Fairly early I was lucky that Professor Beery's system turned out to be so good. I had no one to teach me about "breaking" horses and I saw his ad for the Beery School of Horsemanship in a magazine. It turned out to be a set of booklets—instructions on educating a colt to get him ready for driving and riding and how to continue that education. (The booklets were first copyrighted in 1934 and are still advertised in horse magazines, although the revised edition is not as good as the original.) Professor Jesse Beery understood horses very well and his principles were very sound.

My next "formal" training was with a California vaquero, Bert Allen, who was also a master at starting and riding colts. These two men agreed in principle, educating the colts step by step before and after mounting. While I have added longeing to my repertoire and use some of Professor Beery's and most of Bert's methods, the principles remain the same.

I feel the need to explain my methods to you because they are logical and they are safe. They also can be used successfully by people with less-than-perfect understanding of horses—which includes all of us in varying degrees. I want to offer you and your colt something more humane and less dangerous than many of the methods others expound.

Ideally, the only people who should start colts under saddle are those with above average riding ability. This includes not only the ability to stay balanced on the horse's back and avoid falling off most of the time in explosive situations but also the ability to feel the horse's movements and the degrees of contact with his mouth. This person should also have an intuitive understanding of horses that's well developed through experience and observation.

One big problem with the green rider is that his hands are not steady and so not tactful. When a colt, or any horse, is bugged in the mouth, he can't concentrate on his lessons or his work. It also worries lots of horses to have a rider bouncing on his back or getting off balance. Beginners just aren't ideal colt riders.

The ideal is seldom attainable. This doesn't mean that the less-accomplished horseman is doomed to failure. Through patient and thoughtful application of sound methods he can succeed, just as the more-practiced horseman can fail through overconfidence or misguided methods.

My advice to green riders is to first get a gentle, well-trained horse, learn to ride and understand him, then try to train a colt if that is your dream. But my advice isn't always heeded. I've had people write, "I just love your problem horse book and find it very helpful. I'm a new rider and I bought a two-year-old that I'm going to train myself." My first advice in *There Are No Problem Horses—Only Problem Riders* is that a green rider/colt combination is one of the main causes of problems.

But we all have freedom of choice and we all have to start fulfilling our dreams sometime. If you just can't wait and so ignore my advice on gaining riding experience first, then please listen to my advice on how to proceed patiently and thoughtfully. Your safety and the colt's good education are at stake.

2
Well Equipped

The tools needed for starting a colt are simple but quite definite. They are: a strong halter and a fifteen-foot tie rope with no snap, a snaffle bridle, fifteen- to sixteen-foot driving lines, a saddle you are comfortable with and that doesn't hurt a horse's back, and saddle blankets, of course. No tiedowns, draw reins, or other gimmicks are needed. I'll discuss optional equipment where appropriate. *It is advisable to wear a hard hat.*

Today's nylon halters are best, either flat or round braided. Leather halters are more easily broken. I never use a snap in the tie rope because it can easily break or bend. While nylon ropes are quite strong, it is more difficult to get knots to stay tied in them. I prefer a five-eighths'-inch tightly twisted cotton rope so I don't have to be checking to see that my horse is still tied up. A half-inch nylon rope that is soft and pliable will work if you make sure the knots are holding. We never plan to force the colt to test this equipment, but we want to be sure it will hold him if he does.

A snaffle bridle or a rawhide bosal hackamore is the only thing to use on his head. Most of you will want to use the snaffle. In chapter 14 I discuss the selection and use of the hackamore. *A true snaffle is a bit with ring cheeks.* It may have a variety of mouthpieces including straight bar, twisted wire, double broken, and even something resembling a bicycle chain that is usually called a "mule" bit—poor, misunderstood mules! The single broken mouthpiece that is fairly thick is the best bit. The ring cheeks can be plain, D-ring, or egg-butt. *No curb bit should ever be used on a colt.*

Curb bits include the mechanical hackamore and all those with shanks no matter how long or short. The most cruel bit of all is the so-called western snaffle. This is the shanked bit with the broken mouthpiece that acts as a nutcracker on the horse's bars when tightened by the reins. Curb bits not only are too severe, they twist in the colt's mouth or on his nose as you turn him with the reins. Hurting a colt

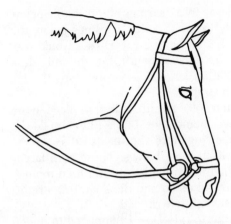

Properly adjusted snaffle bridle and dropped noseband. The dropped noseband should never be lower than this. You should be able to slip two fingers under the chin strap.

or making him uncomfortable, especially in his mouth, can easily trigger behavior that is usually interpreted as "stubborn."

It is good to use a dropped noseband in conjunction with the snaffle bridle if it is adjusted properly. The noseband should be about an inch above the top of the horse's nostrils. The chin strap is buckled below the bit and should never be tightened to keep the horse's mouth closed. You should be able to get two fingers between it and his chin groove. The dropped noseband takes some of the pressure off the horse's bars and puts it on his nose and also prevents pulling the bit through his mouth. However, it is difficult to find one that is made with a short enough nosepiece for most of our horses. Eight to nine inches between the side rings is the right length.

For this reason I recommend a simpler method of keeping the bit in place even though it doesn't relieve any of the pressure on the bars.

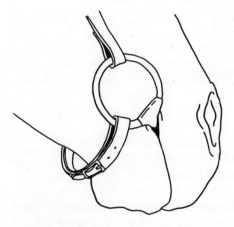

The loose "curb strap" on the snaffle prevents pulling the bit through the horse's mouth.

Fasten a half-inch leather curb strap into the rings of the snaffle below the reins. It should hang loosely but not so that it comes below the horse's chin. I was always told that an egg-butt or D-ring would prevent the bit's slipping through the horse's mouth, but the only time this ever happened to me was with a large-ring egg-butt snaffle. It's so simple to add the leather curb strap!

The bit should fit the individual colt's mouth. When in place, none of the mouthpiece inside the rings should show but neither should the horse's lips be pinched in. Measuring from the inside edges of the rings, a five-inch mouthpiece will fit most horses. Those with larger muzzles will need a five-and-a-half to five-and-a-quarter-inch mouthpiece. When the bridle is properly adjusted and the snaffle sits right, the corners of his lips will be just slightly wrinkled.

One time when I was preparing to ride Dos, I happened to notice that the corners of his mouth were wrinkled excessively. "I couldn't have adjusted the bit that way!" I gasped to myself. I lowered it a notch—still wrinkled badly. Twice more I lowered it with no results, and then Dos opened his mouth and let the bit fall. He had been holding it up high himself, so I put the adjustment back where I originally had it and put it out of my mind.

The size and type of reins are important. I prefer leather or latigo reins with the snaffle. They can be buckled on, end in snaps to snap on, or be laced into the rings by various methods. Whatever method of attachment, they should be three-quarter-inch or seven-eighths'-inch in width to fit your hands comfortably and give you the most secure grip. They also give the proper amount of weight to aid in the mutual feel you and your colt should have between your hands and his mouth. I prefer open reins, each about five feet long. Closed reins are fine if you ride a saddle without a horn to catch the loop on. Their total length should be about nine and a half feet.

Nowadays I see many western riders attaching round braided nylon rope to the snaffle rings with long, wide pieces of leather. These are folded around the snaffle rings where you normally attach the reins. The rope is threaded through a slot in the doubled leather and tied with a sheet bend. This is how the vaqueros attached a mane hair mecate to the snaffle. However, the problem with today's riders is that they use far too big a piece of leather, which causes too much concentrated weight on the bit. Some weight is essential but too much is a pain on the horse's bars.

Because I recommend ground-driving a colt, driving lines are needed. Here again they should have some weight to them for that mutual feel. For this reason two nylon longe lines are not acceptable. My own lines are a pair of single draft horse lines seven-eighths'-inch wide that buckle into the bit. These are not too heavy for most horses but could be for one with an extrasensitive mouth and were for my

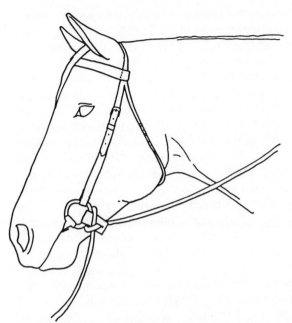

The vaquero method of attaching a mecate to the snaffle. The knot is a sheet bend. The folded leather tab should be small to avoid too much weight on the bit.

Shetland pony. Two half-inch cotton ropes with snaps attached at one end will have good weight and be easy on your hands. Driving lines should always be open-ended so you don't get caught in the loop. Fifteen to sixteen feet each is the right length.

I don't care whether you use a western saddle or some type of "flat" saddle in this venture—just so you are comfortable with your choice and can stay on under most circumstances. It isn't educating a colt properly to keep getting dumped off. Saddle blankets or pads are largely a matter of choice so long as they adequately protect the horse's back. However, those thick, fleecy pads are a poor choice because they don't let a horse's back breathe properly and don't let the saddle hug his back—a thing that makes feeling your horse under you more difficult. I have never found anything better than all wool, woven blankets—two or three thicknesses. If you use a hair pad with the hair exposed, it is advisable to use one thickness of wool blanket between it and the horse. I have found some horses that are quite sensitive to the hair pad and even bucked because of it.

Besides the proper equipment, you need a safe place to handle and ride the colt. Ideally, this is a round corral 50 feet in diameter that opens into an arena 50 to 70 feet wide by 100 to 150 feet long. A square corral about 50 feet each way will work, too, but there a colt can get stuck in the corner seeing a fence with each eye and thinking he has nowhere to go.

The fence of the corral should be at least six feet high. While we try to avoid causing a colt to try to flee, it can happen quite suddenly and for no immediately apparent reason. The high fence helps to discourage him from trying to go over or through it. It also helps in his introduction to turning and stopping since he can't easily get his head over it.

The fence material should be strong, such as two-inch planks spaced four inches apart and six- to eight-inch posts set about eight feet apart. The two-by-four-inch wire mesh horse fencing will work nicely, but it makes it difficult if that is where you tie up the colt. Fencing material must be on the inside of the posts so it isn't easily knocked off. The arena fence should be at least four feet high but need not be such heavy material. This fence is more a psychological barrier to the horse than one to hold a bronc.

This is an expensive setup that probably wouldn't be justified if you have just one or two family colts to start. However, the fifty-foot corral is essential for safety and always useful and so a good investment. Or you can rent steel panels to make up this corral for those first seven to ten days' work.

There are alternatives to the arena. A barn lot or paddock large enough to give you some riding room is suitable. The fence corner of larger fields gives you two fences to help control the colt. The side of the barn or a hedgerow six or more feet high can help in teaching him to turn and stop. You can use any fairly flat area that isn't cluttered with hazards such as tree limbs barely high enough for him to duck under or decorative fence to tangle his feet in or dangerous objects to run into.

The footing doesn't have to be like that of a prepared arena but shouldn't be strewn with boulders or slippery with mud or wet manure. Of course, a cactus patch can quickly make a good rider out of you, but I don't really recommend it!

If you have access to a good setup at a friend's place, a riding club, or a public arena, you might consider making use of it. You would need to haul your colt there to groom him and lead him around enough times to get him used to the place. Otherwise, you will have difficulty getting his attention. Also, you must be able to use it at regular times when others are not. Too much other activity can be very distracting for both you and your colt.

You need a good, safe place to tie up the colt. Cross-ties are handy for grooming but are not suitable for this basic education as they can increase a colt's panic if he gets too nervous. We try very hard to avoid this, but once in awhile it can happen quite unexpectedly. We prepare for the worst and work hard to achieve the best.

Well-set posts of the round or square corral provide a safe place to tie him up. If you are going to make do with what facilities you have, you must find or build a tying place. A strong, solidly set post in a strong board fence will work. Such a post set about four inches from the side of the barn is good. It isn't desirable to use a tree or post out in the open because the colt can go around it, snub himself up short, and panic.

Here at my place I have a large live oak tree that is a cluster of five large trunks that grow close enough together that it makes an ideal place to tie a colt. I take a wrap with the rope around the center trunk above a limb and tie the end of the rope to an outer trunk, so I can reach it without getting near the colt if I have to untie him because of trouble.

There are four knots I use in starting colts that every horseman should know. These are the bowline, the slipknot, the figure eight knot, and the sheet bend. The drawings show how to tie them. I'll explain how to use them as the need arises.

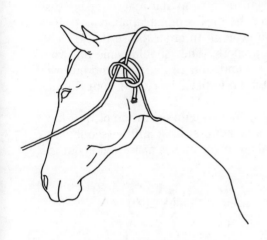

The bowline should be tied snug when the horse's head is at rest. This is a useful knot that won't slip and is easy to untie.

I like the figure eight knot on the halter because it doesn't work loose and is still easy to untie.

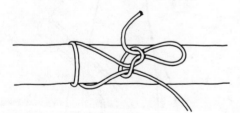

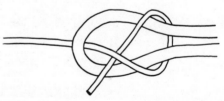

The slipknot—useful when you want to untie it easily. The extra wrap around the post keeps it from pulling too tight to release easily.

The sheet bend is used to tie two ropes together, a line to a sail, and in our case a head to a tail. All knots should be pulled snug to complete their tying.

3
The Aids

Proper rein aids are essential in riding a horse and even more so in starting a colt because they are the means of explanation as well as communication. In order to use the reins effectively, you must hold them properly. They should come into your hands between your little fingers and your ring fingers and out over the tops of your pointers. Hold them in place by closing your thumbs firmly on top of them.

Hold your hands thumbs up with a straight extension of your forearms. Your elbows must always be bent, at least a little (see illustrations). Your hands should be about eight inches apart and about the

Reins come in near the bottom and out under your thumbs—fists closed but not clenched except to tighten the reins briefly. Thumbs up and straight wrists make softer hands.

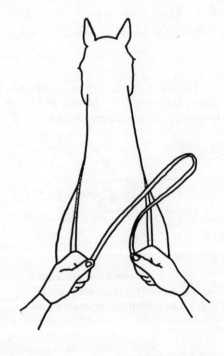

height of your waist. Holding your hands higher than this will cause the horse to stick his nose up in the air. Holding them lower than this will destroy the flexibility of your arms and can cause you to lean forward, putting you out of balance with the colt.

Rein aids range all the way from a subtle tightening of the reins—achieved by closing your fingers a quarter of an inch—to varying degrees of "pull," which is done by moving your whole arm back from your shoulder. It is essential that your fists be closed and relaxed. This is not a tea social. Dainty hands do not make light hands.

With your fingers relaxed and just touching the palms of your hands, you can see that they move that quarter of an inch when you squeeze with them. Your elbow and shoulder joints must also be relaxed so that all use of the reins is gradual and smooth. It is also important to remember that all application of the reins is always followed immediately by smoothly easing off. These are the things that make light hands.

Most people instinctively turn a horse with a direct pull on the inside rein (the left rein in a left turn and vice versa). While this can work on a trained horse, it can cause a colt to set his jaw against the bit, turn his head the opposite way, or bend his neck in the direction of the turn while continuing straight ahead.

The direct rein. *If more than a squeeze is needed, use those wonderful joints in your arm to bring your hand straight back.*

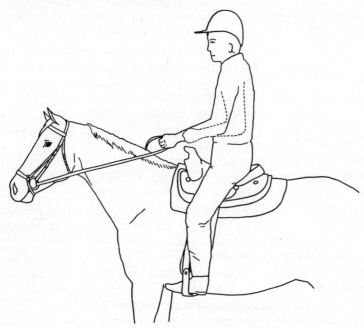

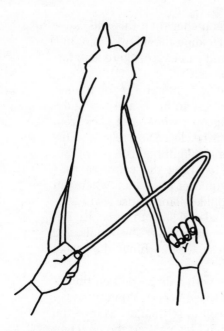

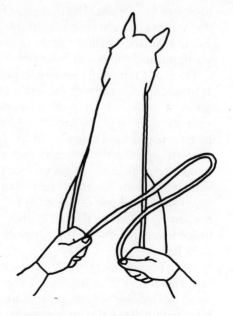

The leading rein *is easily understood by the colt and can smoothly vary from light to strong. Simply roll your hand out from the elbow.*

The indirect rein *brings the rein closer to the horse's neck to turn him without restricting his movement. Use it after the leading rein has taught him to turn.*

Taking the rein straight back is called a *direct rein*. In educating a colt to turn when ridden, you must use a *leading rein*. This is taking the rein out to the side so it leads the colt to turn as if you were standing beside him on the ground. You simply roll your forearm out to the side from your elbow. Your hand will turn so your fingernails are up.

The motion should be smooth and go only as far as necessary. You don't just hold your arm out there at the point where the colt starts turning but work it back and forth slightly so there is take and give—smoothly without jerking. As the colt is completing his turn, you bring your arm back to its normal position.

The other rein aid everyone should know is the *indirect rein*. This is bringing the inside rein slightly closer to the horse's neck as you tighten the rein for a turn. You can achieve this by rolling your hand so the thumb points at the horse's outside ear and your fingernails are up or by simply moving your hand toward the outside side of the horse.

Use the indirect rein in all turns after the colt understands to turn. Even then resort to the leading rein when he fails to obey. His turns will be much smoother if you use the indirect rein instead of the direct rein on the inside, but you can't expect him to respond consistently to it instead of the leading rein for quite some time.

While thousands of horses learn to respond quite well when the rider makes minimum use of his legs, all horses learn to respond better when the rider uses his legs properly. Your legs should always rest against the horse's sides in the girth area. Any squeeze or kick should be straight in, never toward the rear as that raises your seat out of the saddle.

In riding on a circle and through turns, you should always move your outside leg back about two inches. Do this by bending your knee. This helps hold the horse's haunches from drifting out and so helps him bend to the arc of the circle or turn. In stopping you should always squeeze lightly with your legs to help the horse stop in balance. You apply your legs in the same way you do the reins—with a squeeze and release over and over—never with a steady grip.

All of these moves should become reflex action to you. If you have to stop and think to do them, you won't be feeling the horse and responding to his actions or, better yet, to the indications of what his actions will be. A good horseman is constantly responding to the horse in subtle ways without conscious thought. This is another reason why it is better to get lots of educated riding experience before attempting to start a colt.

The most important thing about aids, besides the fact that you should stay relaxed so you can apply them properly, is that you should always say "Please" just before applying them. Even if you must apply them quickly, you should never apply them suddenly. First give a little squeeze with your legs as you take slightly on the reins. Then apply the aids. That little warning—called a half-halt—gets the horse's attention so he is receptive to the ensuing signals. It is saying "Please." Relaxing the aids as he starts to obey is saying "Thank-you."

A The normal position of the leg "on the girth." Your legs should just rest on the horse's sides, your feet just rest in the stirrups.
B The back position of the leg used to hold the horse's haunches in place or move them over. Just bend your knee to move your lower leg back.

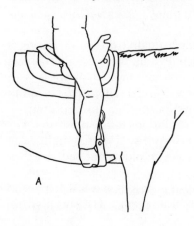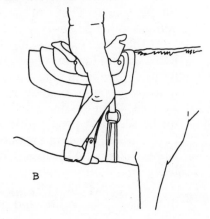

4
Mutual Trust

Perhaps the most important thing to develop in working with your horse is mutual trust. From the first day you handle him, you can build his trust in you by your philosophy, demeanor, and methods. As he grows in understanding and obedience, your trust in him will grow.

Your philosophy concerning horses will determine your demeanor—the way you move and speak around a horse. Good methods in handling a horse are based on the proper philosophy and good understanding of how horses think and react. Each species has its own behavior patterns, its own way of reacting to its environment. In order to get a horse to understand you and react the way you want, you must "speak his language."

There are those whose philosophy toward horses is that they are nothing but dumb animals who must be taught to fear the handler. These people feel they must move right in on a horse to get him under complete control with excessive restraining devices. Their philosophy is, "All training is punishment and reward." That is, force him until he does what you want and then reward him by stopping the force. The cover horse I mentioned in chapter 1 was being handled by men with this philosophy. They can succeed with many horses but also spoil lots of them in the process.

At the other extreme are those who wouldn't dream of hitting a horse for any reason. These people usually talk only in philosophical terms, believing the horse will repay their submissive kindness with undying devotion and cooperation. A few even go so far as to condemn as cruel any of the mechanics necessary for the successful training of the horse. These people write to me for solutions to the problems they have created. Those of the punish-and-reward school of thought don't write so often, not because they don't have problems but because they blame the "dumb, stubborn" horse.

The correct philosophy toward a horse is based on his social structure, his inborn nature, and his physical attributes. His social structure is well organized. There are boss horses, submissive horses, and a pecking order for all those inbetween. He is well acquainted with discipline from colthood on. His mother will physically reprimand him for being too rough, his peers will joust with him, and his superiors can get downright rough if he's too forward or pesty. So he does understand justified punishment that fits the crime.

The horse is amenable by nature—he'd rather flee than fight. This is basically true even though it will be less evident in some individuals. I do believe that outlaws are made most of the time, although there are a few who may be born that way. If you explain to the horse what you want, he is willing to do it to the best of his ability. Horses do vary in nature from just plain lazy to overly energetic, but that just means you have to adapt your methods of explaining to him what you want. He is capable of thinking in horse language, of taking advantage of a situation, and of being respectful. He may fight back if cornered.

A horse appears to be a big, strong animal that should be able to do just about anything. This sort of thinking leads some people to believe that anything one horse can do, all horses can do. This leads to many disappointments in handling horses. They have varying physical talents, and these should always be taken into consideration. Even in starting the colt, we must evaluate the quality of the colt's response according to his individual physical abilities.

Correct philosophy toward horses and handling them must be based on these things: understanding his nature, making use of his social structure, and respecting his physical abilities and limitations. Neither brute force nor maudlin love will get the desired results. Only through treating him as a horse will you gain his complete trust.

This leads us to demeanor—the way you handle yourself to treat the horse as a horse. To do this you must understand how a horse thinks. You must know what his actions and expressions mean and how he reacts to these in other horses. Expecting a horse to think like a human being and to react in the same way can easily lead to your misunderstanding of his motives and his of yours. This leads to mistrust.

While horses do talk to each other vocally, a greater amount of their communication is in body language. Many of these signals are quite obvious—a head thrown up at attention, a rump swung rapidly into kicking position, a head swung at a neighbor, charging another horse, or simply running in play or away from danger. Slight variations in body attitude can make great differences in the meanings of these movements. A colt may suddenly swing his rump toward an older horse in what looks very much like a threat to kick, but the way he squats and extends his neck identifies it as an act of submission.

Watch a group of horses lined up at a feed trough. Without missing a bite, a horse may take a step moving his rump closer to his neighbor. His neighbor will step away if possible or back out to look for a new

It is important to be able to read the horse's body language to know what he is thinking of doing. This colt is expressing submission.

spot if he is hampered by an aggressor on the other side. For a stronger horse the step isn't necessary; he merely eats closer and closer to where his neighbor is eating or briefly flattens his ears. The horses have learned through experience what these movements mean and who is to be obeyed.

The boss horse at the head of a file of horses will swing his head to tell a contender to get back in line or will step from side to side to prevent his getting up alongside. An impatient horse will nip the slow-poke in front of him to get him moving. If a horse in a group raises his head at attention, his companions will respond accordingly—tense and ready for flight if that is the initiator's attitude or merely interested if it is a languid attention.

If a horse is acting nervous and jittery, those around him will begin to get nervous; while a calm horse in a group can help calm the others down with his nonchalant attitude. Knowing this can help you select a fitting companion as a role model for your colt. It also helps you know how to behave around horses.

A horse's body language expresses what he is thinking of a thing or an action and even what he intends to do. Some of these signs are quite subtle. Some are more easily felt than seen at first, but experience can help you recognize them visually as well as through feel and vice versa. I can quickly sense the horse's tense muscles when he thinks of running, bucking, shying, or jumping. From experience and consideration of the circumstances and surroundings, I recognize slight differences that tell me which of these he is planning on executing.

Knowing as soon as the horse does what he is thinking of doing is essential to all handling and training. It makes it possible for you to prevent or encourage the action according to its desirability. Getting the desired behavior from a horse is greatly hampered if you can't prevent the undesired. It is also greatly hampered, perhaps more so, if you mistakenly prevent his doing what you want because you didn't "hear him say" he was going to do it.

You need to become fully aware of a horse's body language, not only to understand him but to help him understand you. He pays more attention to your body language than to your words and interprets in horse terms, not human terms. Making use of this knowledge makes training the horse easier and helps you avoid breaches of horse etiquette.

Your general movements around horses should always be matter-of-fact and deliberate. This reassures the horse that all things are normal. If you rush around, the horse will feel the haste and get nervous. If you are jittery, he will get apprehensive. If you approach him hesitantly, he will think either there is danger lurking nearby or you are a submissive colt he can take advantage of. If you move lazily, he may decide it must be his day of rest.

While a horse does learn verbal commands through consistent association, he automatically pays attention to tone of voice. A wheedling voice makes him think, "I don't have to respect this one. I'm the boss." A loud, roaring voice not only hurts his ears, it makes him wonder if the boss will attack him physically. Lowering your voice—in tone not volume—at the end of a command helps slow him down. Raising it at the end helps activate him. You can express displeasure through short, sharp words but need not and should not shout. And he understands the tone of a genuinely felt "Good boy!"

While the horse does intuitively get the feel of these various tones of voice, appropriate aids used in conjunction with them will reinforce his instincts. There is one tone of voice or method of speaking he will understand completely and that is matter-of-fact. It goes hand in hand with your matter-of-fact way of moving.

If we aren't aware of a horse's body language, we can inadvertently threaten him. Approaching a horse too rapidly threatens him. Approaching in any manner straight at his head expresses threat to him. Your approach should always be deliberate and toward his shoulder. If he shows signs of agitation, it is better to stop briefly as a means of reassuring him than to proceed hesitantly.

He is especially aware of hand movements and tense muscles. Keep your body relaxed and your hands quiet. A quick hand movement toward his head means the same thing to him as another horse's slinging his head in his direction—"Get out of my way or I'll clobber you!" On the other hand, a threatening hand or a quick swat can be effective punishment since he equates it with a normal horse reprimand. These

The quick movement of your hand toward a horse's head means the same thing to him as

another horse swinging his head to tell him to get back in line.

should be used only for unsocial behavior, not for seeming refusal to do what you are trying to teach him. That calls for a better explanation so he can understand what you want.

Making proper use of equine social behavior helps to build his trust. He thinks of you as a horse and respects you for applying equine rules. For example, scratching a horse at his withers means the same thing to him as "chewing manes"—the horses' mutual acts of social acceptance. In fact, he may try to respond by "chewing your mane"—a thing to be tactfully discouraged because his teeth are big, his jaws are strong, and horsehide is tougher than yours.

So develop the proper philosophy. Remember that horses are smart if you rate their IQs as horses instead of humans. Bear in mind that you are to be the wise leader and teacher as a horse, not a bullying human tyrant. Be aware that horses take advantage of their wishy-washy equine companions, that they respect justified reprimands from their superiors, that they much prefer to be treated as horses.

Practice the proper demeanor around all horses. If horses didn't want some members of their band to be the guide and mentor, they would go their separate ways. Those guides and mentors hold their places in horse society through their calm and firm approach to daily living. Make yourself that kind of horse.

Select training methods that are sound from the horse's point of view. Ask yourself, "Does this method explain to the horse what I want in his language and in logical steps of development?" How you apply any method must take into consideration the individual's basic ability and his stage of development, both mental and physical.

There is an important rule to follow in training colts and teaching any horse any new thing. *Give him time to understand, time to respond, and time to get in the habit.* Immediate response to any command comes only after the horse is thoroughly practiced in the maneuver.

These things all add up to respect for the horse as a horse. They build mutual trust. I would rather have a less-than-perfectly-trained horse who trusts me than a robot who performs beautifully if I push the right buttons. The horse that trusts me will go to great lengths to do what I ask of him even if it is scary.

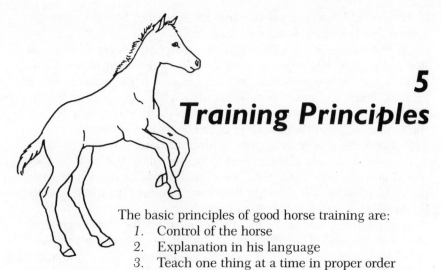

5
Training Principles

The basic principles of good horse training are:
1. Control of the horse
2. Explanation in his language
3. Teach one thing at a time in proper order
4. Reinforce learned behavior through consistent repetition
5. Avoid confrontation

You can't teach a horse anything if you can't control him. While control must be physical by various methods, it is also essential that it be psychological. The horse must think you are stronger than he is. Even more important, he must accept you as the boss horse—the leader who must be obeyed. Minimal physical controls applied with the proper leverage can convince him that you are stronger and are to be listened to. Even subtle use of his own language will reinforce his conviction that you are his superior.

You can't teach a horse anything if you can't control him.

Using necessary means to control a horse trains him psychologically as well as physically.

You can control a foal by leading his mother, by containing him in a stall, by your strength applied to restrain him but not hurt him, and by using techniques rather than force to teach him to lead. You can control a horse walking away from you by stepping to one side so he sees you with just one eye and so turns away. You can wave your hand at the right moment to stop and turn him and can continue this until he will stand still so you can walk up to him, if he is also controlled by a small corral. These things combine psychological and physical control.

When you tie up a horse with strong equipment in a safe place, you have physical control over him. If you step back and let him try it out for himself, he soon learns to accept the limitations and doesn't blame you for any discomforts experienced in the learning. We always try to arrange these types of controls so the colt inflicts the discomfort on himself.

When you use the leverage of turning a horse's head to the side as he tries to bolt during leading, you not only have controlled him but have made him think you are stronger than he is. This enhances your image as head honcho without a battle. You need the means to control the colt so you can explain to him what you want him to do and to build your image as trusted friend and master.

I have talked to you about using the horse's language in explaining things to him and about how he interprets your language. Besides body language and tones of voice, there are ways of using controls and positioning the colt to help him understand what you want and make it possible for him to do it. I will explain these as each occasion arises.

There is one thing you shouldn't do in any language and that is try to fool him. He might very well enjoy sneaking up on a buddy and goosing him, but he won't appreciate your trying to sneak him into a situation that is strange to him. Always let him see what is happening and explain it to him in a way he can understand that he won't be hurt.

I have seen people try to hurry a horse into a trailer "before he can realize what is happening." This is doomed to failure because of the hurried attitude and because horses are very quick to assess a strange situation as potentially dangerous. I have seen people try to sneak a saddle on a colt's back only to have him jump away from the strange feel or quickly dump it when he caught sight of the strange object now perched on his back.

I watched one trainer cover a colt's near eye while the rider carefully mounted from a high step so the saddle wouldn't twist and pinch. The colt walked off a few strides, felt the twist and pinch of the cinch, caught sight of the rider high above him, and bucked her off. To paraphrase Thelwell, they took him back, reassured the rider, and made them do it again—which they both did.

I did deliberately fool a horse one time. I had to doctor a wound on Swede's hind leg. At the mere sight of the medicine bottle, he started to dance a jig. He had an old scar on him and apparently had a mental trauma about doctoring. I quickly discovered I could touch the wound without his flinching while I was brushing his leg. Since the medicine was soothing, not stinging, I doctored him several times while brushing him. It was so funny, too, because after one such doctoring was completed, he saw me pick up the medicine bottle and started to dance that jig. I lovingly laughed at him and told him he was already doctored.

This type of fooling was successful *only* because I knew ahead of time that he accepted my touching the wound during brushing and because he would not be shocked by medicine that inflicted sudden pain, sudden cold, or the tickle of a spray. Swede soon let me doctor him without the fooling. Fooling or attempting to fool a horse in any way that will end up in mental or physical shock to him is just inviting trouble.

It is of utmost importance that the horse trust you. Give the horse a chance to see things, and even feel them with his nose. Don't threaten him with equipment by suddenly thrusting it at or on him. Approach in a matter-of-fact sort of way or, better yet, let his curiosity bring him to you and the objects. This explains in his language that these things won't hurt him, and your deliberate movements in touching him with them furthers that explanation. Just don't think for a minute that you can fool him.

A horse can eventually do more than one thing at a time but he can't learn it all at once. Neither can he learn a more difficult thing without first learning the foundation for doing it. While you must teach go, turn, and stop in the same lesson, you obviously shouldn't ask the colt to go while you are pulling on the reins. That is giving him conflicting signals. Also, you shouldn't ask him to turn at the same time you ask him to start going. That is teaching two things at

Make use of the horse's natural curiosity to introduce him to strange things and to avoid threatening him. Gaining his trust is essential for a lifetime of good relations.

a time. Consistent repetition means you ask him with the same signals each time and reward him for the same good performance. This establishes your language in his mind and his consistent obedience to your requests.

While there are times when a colt must be "put in his place," we try to avoid confrontation in the learning process. It is very unproductive to start a fight as the colt is then in no frame of mind to understand you or try to do what you ask. Losing your temper is one of the best ways to start a losing fight with your horse. If you feel frustration causing you to lose your cool, take a breather. If that doesn't work, ask the colt to do some simple thing he does well, pet him, and put him away.

Confrontation can take place without the trainer's realizing it. He can actually be asking the colt to learn two things instead of just one. Or he may not realize that the colt isn't understanding his explanation and so try to force the issue. He may try to further initial success by asking for immediate repetition. Many times I've said, "We finally did it! Let's do it again." It's that "finally" that's the clue. If it took long enough to evoke that word, then both of you are tired and will blow it if you ask again. Stop right there, pet the horse, and put him away. It will pay off with continuing success in the next lesson.

Right here is a good place to put to rest that false notion that you must get the colt to do what you started to teach him before you stop the lesson. Time and again I have stopped trying to teach a horse something, gone back to some other thing he could do well so I could praise him for it, and then put him away. Time and again, though not always, the horse has done that difficult thing the first time I asked the following day.

A colt can get tired, he can get confused, his brain can get numb. In this condition he is incapable of learning, and you can spoil much that has been accomplished already by insisting that he learn some specific thing just because you started to teach it to him. Going back to something he can do well gives you a chance to put him away on a good note. The chances are very good he will think it over with his feed and have the right answer at the next lesson. There is also a good chance you will think it over with your feed and have the right answer, too!

Training Principles   25

6
Preschool

No colt should be ridden before he is two and a half years old. He may be a strapping big colt and you may be a small person, but it isn't so much the weight on his back that is the problem but the fact that he can easily make a false move and injure his underdeveloped joints. Also, his length of concentration is very short. This is why I don't bother with saddling and ground driving until I am ready to go on with the riding.

There are plenty of things you can do before that time that will make your work easier when it is time to start his education in being ridden. He should learn to stand tied patiently, lead well from both sides, accept grooming and having his feet picked up. These indoctrinate him in simple obedience and in the joys of your companionship. While cross-ties are handy in working around a horse, they should not be used when doing the work connected with starting the colt because they are too unstable. If you use cross-ties, also be sure your colt will stand tied to a solid post.

If you don't know how to train a colt to tie up, lead, and pick up his feet, I feel you aren't qualified to train a colt to be ridden. However, let me tell you a little bit about these things so you don't make serious mistakes.

The rules for tying up an unbroken colt are the same as those for tying him for his saddle training: use strong equipment to tie him to a strong post in a safe place, and tie him at least six inches above wither height (see chapter 7). It is essential that he never learns he can break loose; he should be tied up daily for a week or more so he learns the lesson thoroughly.

The only difference in these initial tying lessons is that I like to use a 5/8- or 3/4-inch rope around the colt's body just behind the withers as well as the halter rope. Tie it with a bowline just barely snug around his girth, run the tying end between his front legs and through the nosepiece of the halter, and tie it along with the lead rope. Adjust it initially so it takes hold before the lead rope. Gradually change to let-

In initial tying lessons the body rope effectively holds the colt and lessens the chance of injury to his neck.

ting the lead rope take hold first and finally to eliminating the body rope.

Never use cross-ties to train a colt to stand tied. They easily create a panic situation for him. After he is well trained to stand tied, get him used to cross-ties by snapping one side to the halter and snapping a lead rope into the opposite ring instead of the other cross-tie. By varying his freedom with this rope you can gradually indoctrinate him to the restriction of cross-ties. In them a horse should always be able to take a step forward and back and turn his head at least a foot to each side.

In training a foal to lead I like to use a longer lead rope so I can form a rump rope with its end by holding the end and the rope together to form the loop. It gives me more freedom to dispense with it if necessary. A rump rope should always be used with short tugs, never a steady pull. When the foal steps forward, the rope should loosen as a reward. The tug tells him to step forward.

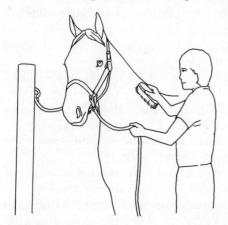

By using the lead rope in place of the second cross-tie, you can train the horse gradually to accept more restriction.

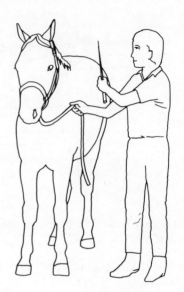

Teach him to step forward when tapped on top of his hips, with the whip in this position. Bring the whip up and forward every time you stop him.

You want the foal—and the older horse—to step forward with you rather than merely be towed along on the lead rope. For this reason I like to use the whip to train the older colt. Stand beside his shoulder with a little slack in the lead rope. With the whip in your left hand turn it back over your right shoulder to tap him on top of his hips. Make each tap a little harder until he takes a step. Immediately raise the whip and pet him.

When he understands to step forward as the whip touches his hips, walk forward with him with the whip in that position. Each time he slows down, tap him. To stop him, turn the whip up and forward and stop yourself so he runs into the braced lead rope. When he leads easily this way, you can dispense with the whip.

Remember, in picking up his feet you are training him to pick them up rather than let you pick them up. He will lift a front foot if you lean into his shoulder to encourage him to shift his weight to the other foot and you pinch down the tendon at the back of his cannon. For a hind foot lean into his rump and slide your hand down the back tendon of the cannon with a forward and upward pressure.

Take this training one step at a time. First praise him for just lifting his foot, then get him to let you hold it up for gradually longer periods. Be sure you are the one who tells him to put it down but never just drop it. Let him know by a wiggle and a little support that you are letting it down. With the hind feet gradually work them toward the rear after he lets you hold them up without a struggle.

When the colt is leading well, you can also take him around the premises to get him acquainted with the man-made environment. Use judgment in this. Don't expect him to stand quietly beside a truck that suddenly roars to life or not try to run away if some unidentified foreign object comes toward him. You can lead a colt up to a strange thing (with patience), but you can't expect him to wait around when a UFO appears to be attacking him by coming toward him. However, if you lead him to follow a car going away from him, it will help get him used to traffic.

One good way to further his education is to tie him up beside your saddle horse while you are preparing him for riding. (This is true only if your saddle horse is well behaved.) When I lived at Oak Run, our horses ran loose and both Coltburger and our pony colt, Jackrabbit, would come to stand at the hitching rail when we were getting our saddle horses ready to ride. We would give them turns at being brushed and even occasionally place a saddle blanket on their backs. We made sure not to startle them in this and they not only accepted it but were quite proud to be treated like "older" horses. Horses do learn from each other. For this reason it's wise to keep colts away from "outlaws."

Ideally, once a colt has learned to stand tied, lead, and be handled all over, the best education he can get is running in hilly country with other horses. There he can learn to respect his elders and interact with his peers. He can develop bone and muscle and agility. All of these

Horses learn from each other. "Outlaws" can be a bad influence, well-behaved horses a big help.

things make him a better saddle horse in the long run. Even if he can't run under such ideal conditions, I feel it is better to let him be the baby horse he is to the best extent possible than to try to make him into a human companion/servant at such a tender age. It will save you the trouble of having to teach him to move like a horse before you can teach him to use those movements for your benefit.

When I had colts to start, I would spend a month in the fall of their second year giving them the complete basic course. By the end of the month I could ride them out on the trail in walk, trot, and canter. I could turn and stop them easily and they would move along freely, trusting me to keep them out of trouble. I would then turn them loose with the other horses over the winter.

In the spring it took only one or two days to give them a refresher course in saddling and bridling and riding in the corral. Then we were on our way to more serious training. I've had some self-styled experts tell me that once you start riding a colt, you can't lay him off because he will go bad. To me this is just a proof of the poor quality of that person's methods of starting colts.

If this colt you plan to start is one you just bought and he is old enough for the work, don't think you can plunge right into the training. You are a stranger who must be evaluated. Spend a month making sure he ties up, grooming him, and leading him. Show him you can be trusted. I've found that fillies often take a little longer to become trustful than colts do.

This might be a good place to speak of mustangs. My method of starting colts will work very well with them—after you have gone through a getting-acquainted period. A farmer in my home state of Indiana let me in on the secret of "taming" a mustang or range-raised colt. He would tie him up in the barn where it was safe and where the colt could reach his feed and water. The farmer was the only one who would bring that hay and water. He said that in just a matter of days the colt would be looking forward to his coming. Soon he could begin rubbing the colt with his hands and then with brushes.

This is what you should do with your mustang when you get him. Be sure your equipment is strong so he can't break it and the place you tie him is safe for him and for you to approach to feed and later rub him. When he is accepting you in these things, you can then start teaching him to lead in an enclosed area where he can't escape. After he leads well and accepts your handling him and is trusting, you can start him by my method when he is old enough.

If you are having trouble in teaching your colt to tie up, lead, and pick up his feet, you can get the answers to these problems in chapters 15 and 20 of my book *There Are No Problem Horses—Only Problem Riders*. Regardless of his age, it is essential that he will tie up and lead before starting the work that begins in the next chapter.

7
Sacking Out

The terms "sacking out" and "breaking a colt" have suffered the same fate. Those who do them properly use these terms and think nothing of it. Those who have seen these things done improperly abhor the terms as well as the improper applications. By this reasoning, we could also hate "training a horse" or "starting a colt" since there are those who use those terms and still do the job improperly.

So if sacking out causes you to throw up your hands in horror, perhaps you should think of it as "indoctrination." No matter what name you call it, what I mean by sacking out is essential to any horse's good education. It is good education only if it is done properly. This is where philosophy comes in—you don't want the colt to fear you; you want him to trust you because he learns that all the things you do around and to him won't hurt him. You want him to come to believe that these are commonplace things that happen to all horses and that they are harmless.

At the moment you appear on the scene you are sacking out the colt. How you conduct yourself determines whether you are doing it properly or improperly. I hate to see anyone chase a horse of any age around just to see it put on a show or demonstrate its way of moving for a friend or prospective customer. This is improper sacking out.

A colt of ten to thirty days of age can be quietly crowded into a corner and controlled with your body and arms in order to slip the halter on his head. This is proper sacking out. When you scratch a colt on his withers, rub him on his neck and body and legs, and when you groom him, you are sacking him out. You can use a rub rag that you gradually let flop. You can even get him used to fly spray, if you keep one hand on his neck and let him hear the faint hiss steadily before the spray contacts his body, or get him used to water from the hose, if you run it gently in the same area you are rubbing him with your hand.

Just remember in all things you do to avoid threatening him. Don't attack him at his head or breast or with sudden movements. Start in

Everything you do with a horse is sacking him out—for better or worse depending upon how you do it.

the area of his withers or shoulder and gradually rub closer and closer to his head, and soon you'll be able to rub his head and ears. Start over with the brush and soon you can use the soft brush on his head.

Always start the fly spray there at his withers, even after he is used to it, since there is always the chance that the sudden tickle on his breast or neck will startle him. I start the water hose on his legs because water trickling down them from higher up is upsetting to a horse, sometimes forever.

So the work you do with a colt before he is ready to start his saddling education can prepare him for the sacking out that is to come. How you handle this early indoctrination will affect how he responds to the serious sacking out. Did you build his trust or simply insist that he's your colt so he has to accept whatever you want to do with him?

When the colt is two and a half or three years old, it is time to start his saddle training. This begins with sacking out, and the first rule is control. He must be tied in a safe place with strong equipment. With my years of experience I now seldom have a colt pull back, but it can happen quite unexpectedly. It is better to be prepared than to have to back up and cure a halter-breaking problem.

I tie the lead rope into the halter ring with a figure eight knot because it is less likely to come untied than a bowline and is more easily untied than a slipknot. There should be fourteen to eighteen inches of rope between this knot and the post, depending on the size of the pony or horse. Any less than this can panic the colt, any more can let him turn far enough to get in trouble.

At the post, the rope should be tied on a level at least six inches above the height of his withers. If a horse pulls back on a rope tied lower than his wither height, he can pull his neck down. The sudden strain at that angle can cause the tendons to slip off the bones at his withers. If it is very severe, he can no longer raise his head and is ruined.

My saddle horse, Iam, had been a well-trained horse for several years when this happened to him. Because he was very well trained, I no longer tied him at wither height. He was also used to fly spray, but while I was in the house, the horseshoer sprayed him, starting on his breast. For some reason (he may have been asleep), this startled him and he pulled back. A few days later I noticed that he had a dip in front of his withers that hadn't been there before. His neck was pulled down but only enough to make this unsightly dip, not enough to ruin him for life. This is why I now say that all horses should be tied at wither height or above, and all fly spraying should start on the body.

So tie the colt at least six inches above his wither height. When you are tying the rope to the post, take two complete wraps around the post before tying the slipknot. This makes it possible to untie it after a horse has pulled back. I prefer to take one wrap around that post and go to the next post to tie up. This way the slipknot can always be untied and you can get to the post to untie it if the colt gets into serious trouble.

It's a good idea to always carry a sharp pocketknife when working around horses. You never know when it might come in handy. In all my dealings with colts, I think about and prepare for the worst things that could happen and work very hard to avoid them. This keeps me from getting hurt and prevents accidents that will start a bad habit in a colt.

The colt should be tied at least six inches above wither height for his safety. Taking a wrap on one post and tying to the next one over makes releasing him easier in case of trouble.

When I started Iam under saddle, I hadn't done this for several years and had to keep reminding myself that I was working with a colt, not an older, trained horse. He was so gentle and amenable that it tended to lull me into complacency. Even the most gentle colt can be startled into an explosive move, so stay alert to anything that could go wrong and praise the Lord that you have a colt who makes your work so easy.

The paraphernalia you will need for sacking out is a gunnysack, a saddle blanket, and a rope at least ten feet long. Gunnysacks (jute feed bags) are scarce these days, at least in my area. An old pair of jeans would be a good substitute. I also use my work chinks (short chaps) as they are made out of buckskin and so are soft with only a little rattle.

You shouldn't use plastic or a slicker at this time. These things are too scary for a colt and should wait until you have thoroughly established his trust. Iam was well advanced in basic training when I decided one day to longe him instead of riding because the weather looked threatening. Just as I got him to the longe circle, it started to sprinkle. Not wanting to get my saddle wet, I thought I would tie a piece of plastic over it.

I led him back into the stall and started to put the plastic on. His muscles tensed and he pulled his body away from me. "Oh, it scares you," I said in a matter-of-fact tone. I immediately brought it back to my body where he could reach his head around to feel and smell it. I then rustled it a little and proceeded to rub him on the shoulder with it. I could then put it on the saddle.

Iam trusted me but the plastic was noisy and white. Even though I moved it toward his back, he felt threatened. I immediately recognized the signs and "retreated." I let him investigate and proceeded with the indoctrination at his speed. Awareness of the colt's reactions and responsive conduct on your part are very important in sacking out—a thing that can continue throughout the horse's life as the occasion demands.

I've heard of rolling oil drums toward a tied-up colt and turning him loose in the corral with sacks of tin cans hanging on the saddle. I did try the latter one time when I was much younger and greener. It scared the poor fellow out of his wits. Cowboys, when moving a herd, will sometimes rattle pebbles in a tin can to keep the lazy cattle moving. They call it a "tin dog." But the horses have already learned to trust their riders and don't object to that little rattle.

The purpose of sacking out isn't to scare the colt into submission. It is important to monitor his reaction at all times so you can ease off if he is getting too tense. Sometimes you have to stop the rubbing or flopping with the sack or rope and give him another chance to investigate them with his nose and lips so he can reassure himself.

During initial sacking out, I keep one hand on his neck or body so

I can feel as well as see his reaction. This is also reassuring to him and will push me out of the way if he makes a jump in my direction. It is all right if he moves around some, but when he gets bug-eyed and rigid, it is definitely time to stop and let him take a breather so you can start again.

However, during the rubbing and flopping, it is better to go at it steadily, gradually getting stronger and easing off in response to the colt's reactions. If you sack him intermittently, you startle him each time you start again. It is much quicker and better to lull him into acceptance with a steady rhythm, going up and down from pianissimo to fortissimo and back down according to his responses.

I use the gunnysack (or blue jeans) first because it is neutral in color, smells good, and is soft and quiet. With the colt properly tied up, I approach his left side holding the sack in my left hand where he can see it. If he acts scared, I just stop and wait. Soon I can get close enough that he can reach out and smell and feel it with his nose. Then I can transfer it to my right hand, place my left hand on his neck, and start rubbing him with the sack on his withers and shoulder.

As I approach him and while I work, I'm telling him all about it in a matter-of-fact tone of voice. "This is a gunnysack. It smells good. It's just like the rub rag only bigger. Doesn't that feel good?"—just anything good that comes to mind. The vaquero who taught me these things always whistled a steady, tuneless tune softly through his teeth. Talking or the soft whistle serves two purposes—it helps reassure the colt and it lets him know at all times where you are. Your hand on his neck also helps to reassure him and gives you the advantage of feeling if his muscles tense up.

I gradually run the sack over more of his body and with more vigorous motions. It is okay if the colt moves around, but if he tenses up, I keep rubbing but go back toward his withers and ease up on the motions. When he is relaxed about this rubbing and flopping sack, I lay it on his back and leave it there while I go around him to go through the same process on his off side.

The next move is to start flopping the sack up and down beside him and against his body, always keeping your free hand on his neck or shoulder. Start with small movements that gradually get more vigorous. Keep a steady flop, flop, flop, moving the sack closer to make it softer and farther away to make it stronger as his reaction demands. He will quickly get used to it. *Be sure he can see what you are doing.*

If the colt is getting too tense, I do stop briefly and let him smell the sack again. Then I start with the rubbing and work right on up to where we were when he tensed up so much. Almost always he will then accept it.

I flop the sack against his body on top, sides, and underneath; on top of his hips; and against his legs. I only rub it on his neck, breast, and gently up toward his head, where I eventually drape it briefly and then pull it off. It is always the reaction of the colt that tells me how fast I can advance through all this. If he starts going to sleep on the job, it's definitely time to move on to the other side and then to the saddle blanket, although I don't usually wait for this extreme signal—just the indications of acceptance, the air about him that he's saying, "This is okay."

I go through the same steps with the saddle blanket. (A single one is easier to handle than a double.) Now there is more weight that flops on his back and against his sides, but he quickly accepts that if you follow the same rules of steady rhythm and ease off if he gets too tense. As he accepts it on his body, I then flop it high to let it fall on his withers. Soon he must see a saddle raised over his back and then a person rising up above him, so it is good for him to get used to that blanket high up over his withers.

I was helping a friend with a colt that had already been ridden a lot but was too hyper at times. When she lifted the saddle toward his back, he stepped away as far as he could. He didn't get scared, just moved away. I finally said, "This is ridiculous," and took the saddle blanket and sacked him out on and over his back on both sides until he would stand still for it. He then stood for being saddled, not just that one time but in subsequent saddlings.

I flop that blanket all over a colt and leave it on his withers or hips to go to the other side to retrieve it. When I'm fairly confident he won't

Sacking out high over his back prepares him for saddling and mounting. Remember to take an extra wrap before tying the slipknot if you tie to just one post.

Starting the Colt

Pushing the blanket off his hips educates him not to kick when startled. This much reaction the first time is to be expected.

kick, I push it off his hips to fall on the ground beside his hind feet. I put my hand on his hindquarters as I retrieve the blanket from this position and pull it away smoothly. If he acts especially goosey about its falling beside his hind feet, it is better to pull it away with a stick and sack out his hindquarters more before doing it again.

After the blanket comes the rope. I never actually hit him with it but do flop it against him, toss it up and let it fall on him, and toss it out toward his hind feet and let it drag as I coil it up. Be sure he sees it. Briefly stop coiling and dragging if he gets too spooked.

This dragging the rope beside him is important because it will help prevent his getting spooked if at some time he happens to get loose with a rope dragging. This can be quite dangerous to him and to you too if you are caught in the other end of the rope. *But you should avoid that by never putting your arm through the coils of a rope or letting the rope lie coiled on the ground if it is attached to the horse.*

The other thing I do with the rope is toss it so it curls around his legs, especially the hind legs. Practice on a post and you will see that you can make a rope do this without hitting the post hard. The rope just comes in from the side and wraps around. This is the best way I know to cure a horse of wanting to kick, although you can tie the gunnysack on the end of a stick so you can sack out his hind feet without getting in kicking range. On a spooky colt I sack out his hind feet by either method before I shove the blanket off his hips.

It is also a good idea to get a horse to accept a rope under his tail. It is essential to do this if you intend to drive him. When he is accept-

Sacking Out

Tossing the rope from the side makes it coil around his legs without hitting him hard. This too educates him not to kick.

ing the rope and blanket flopped on and around his hindquarters, stand beside him with your hand on his hip and take hold of his tail-bone and lift his tail. (I was told by my vaquero mentor that no horse will kick if you take hold of the tailbone. I have never tried it on a bronc to see if it is true but have found that horses do readily accept it.)

Some horses resist your lifting their tails so you may need to work gently to get him to relax some for this. When you can lift his tail without too much struggle, place a smooth stick crossways under it and let the tail down. This acquaints him with the feel. Next put the rope under his tail. I go from holding it there, to moving it back and forth gently, to pulling it slowly down and away as he relaxes his tail.

The stick and the rope won't bother him much snug up high in the groove at the root of his tail, but he may clamp down on them lower down. Just wait a bit until he relaxes his tail some before moving or pulling away the rope. Lift his tail to remove the stick. Repeat this lesson until he accepts the rope moving under his tail without clamping down on it.

All this can save your getting dumped as I was when the rope accidentally got under the tail of the colt I was riding. I didn't even know what had happened until afterward. I was just suddenly lying on my back on the ground looking up at the colt. No matter how much I tried, I could never get him to accept a rope under his tail after that.

With the colt under control you are explaining to him, one thing at a time, that these things don't hurt him. You will reinforce this edu-

Starting the Colt

He will accept the smooth stick under his tail. After that he can learn to accept the rope.

cation by sacking him out at the beginning of the next few lessons. And you will avoid confrontation by not pushing him beyond what he can stand.

With most colts I can do all this sacking out, then saddle and bridle the colt to turn him loose in the corral all in one lesson. However, if you haven't had enough experience or find it difficult to read a horse's body language, take it more slowly. It doesn't hurt anything to take a week of lessons to cover this much ground. Haste can make problems when handling horses.

8
Saddling, Mounting, and Bitting

When the colt has accepted sacking out, you can put the saddle on him. As I mentioned, I usually do this in the first lesson, but you must not think you have to hurry. First be sure he accepts sacking out with equanimity.

Saddling improperly can cause at least two problems—fear of the saddle and cinchiness. A good horseman never throws the saddle on a horse's back or jerks the cinch up tight. That's movie stuff. *The saddle should always be placed on a horse's back and the cinch or girth should always be taken up smoothly and by degrees.* Failing to follow either procedure even after the colt has accepted the saddle and the cinching can cause the problems you try to avoid.

Laying the cinch and off-stirrup leather across the seat of the saddle and lifting the saddle onto the colt's back is quite acceptable as long as they will stay in place and you can lift high enough to put the saddle in position. From my vaquero teacher I learned a better way that actually takes less strength but can be done only if the saddle has a high enough horn that you can grasp it or an open throat that you can get your hand in.

Lift the saddle with your right hand in the throat of the saddle or around the horn. With your left hand, hold up the off stirrup leather and the cinch just below the saddle skirts. Standing at the horse's shoulder facing the rear, lift the stirrup leather and cinch over the horse's back as you swing the saddle up and over, but just far enough that the off skirts are resting on the horse's back just beyond his spine. Let go with your left hand as the saddle comes into this position.

With the saddle this far into position you can easily hold it there with one hand even if the colt moves around. To put the saddle in place, you take hold of the horn or maintain your hold on it with your right hand. Use the leverage of your hand and elbow and the help of

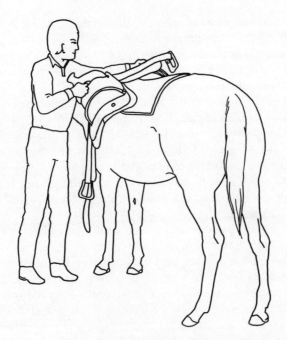

I hold up the cinch and off stirrup leather and swing the saddle up and over to land...

with the off skirts just across the horse's spine. Then I can hold the saddle horn and the front of the near skirt to lift the saddle into place.

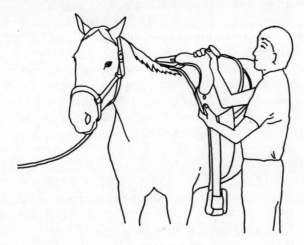

your left hand holding the front of the near skirts to lift the saddle and position it.

I use this method to saddle all horses. I like it because it takes less strength, it doesn't disturb the saddle blankets, and it is easier to set the saddle down in the proper position. I find it very hard to reposition a saddle once it is on except for the little slide back it should always get to lay the hair on the horse's back. If you want to use this method, practice on a trained horse, not on the colt.

When I plan to saddle the colt, I lay the saddle on the ground out of the way a few feet from the tying post. Then when I lead the colt out, if he shows interest in it, I lead him up to it. However, I don't force the issue. If he seems a little leery, I might wait a few minutes for his curiosity to get the better of him and then lead him on up so he can nudge and smell it. If he's too leery, I just tie him up. It isn't a good idea to put the saddle in his stall for him to get acquainted with it as colts can be quite destructive with their teeth.

After tying up the colt and giving him a refresher in sacking out, carry the saddle toward his body in plain view. Stop briefly if he seems overly scared, let him relax, and then proceed. Let him smell and nuzzle it. Rub it on his shoulder and then lift it on his back. I make sure he has accepted it there before I let go of it. When he relaxes, I go to the other side to make sure everything is straight and then come back to cinch up. I don't hurry but I don't waste any time either as I want him to stand until I can get it cinched just snug enough to stay put. I talk quietly to keep any movement he may make to a minimum.

Take the cinch up smoothly until it is just barely tight enough to hold the saddle in place if he jumps around a little. Let him soak up the feel for a bit, then tug several times with your hand under the latigo so he accepts the tighter feel. Don't crowd him into reacting to this; just give him an inkling of things to come. Then you can finish smoothly tightening the cinch to where it should be—just tight enough that you can still squeeze the flat of your hand under it.

Let me put in a note about cinching stock saddles. Quite a few people will pull the cinch snug when they first thread the latigo through the cinch ring. This is a useless maneuver because it can't possibly stay snug, and you need room to take the second wrap. On a colt it can spell disaster. If he jumps at the feel of the snug cinch, he will dump the saddle.

Always let the cinch hang loose on the latigo while you thread it through the rigging ring and down through the cinch ring the second time. Then you can ease the cinch up to snug and it will hold the saddle even if the colt makes a jump or two. Even trained horses can get startled at the wrong moment, so get rid of this useless and accident-prone habit.

Another thing is the double-rigged saddle. I don't like them because they are usually full or seven-eighths rigged, which means the front cinch is almost directly under the fork of the saddle. This positions the saddle farther back on the horse, putting the rider a little behind his

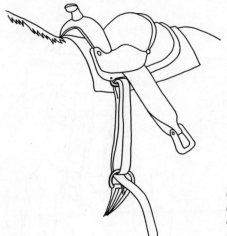

Never pull the cinch up snug until after you have taken this second wrap through the cinch ring. One wrap won't hold and could cause an accident.

center of balance. The back cinch serves no purpose unless you are a roper who does most of his work facing the roped cow or calf.

If you have a double-rigged saddle, always remember to fasten the back cinch last and unfasten it first. It won't hold the saddle in place by itself. The back cinch should always be fastened to the front cinch in the middle so it can go back no farther than six to eight inches. It should always be buckled up just barely snug. If it is left hanging, the horse can get a hind foot in it. If it is too tight, it interferes with his movement.

In saddling the colt, initially take the back cinch up slightly loose and tug on it several times the same as you do on the front cinch. Then after you finish tightening the front cinch, you can make the back one just barely snug.

After taking up the cinch enough and when the colt shows some relaxation, I sack him out again with the gunnysack. Then I wiggle the saddle from both sides and tug more on the latigo. I lift the stirrups away from his sides and let them drop, first a little way and then farther. I want him to get used to the idea that this camel's hump he has acquired does move around, bump him, and pinch him.

In preparation for mounting, I hang on each side of the saddle to let him get the feel of that pinch when I finally put my weight in the stirrup. I make little hops beside him on either side to prepare him for the bounce I must make to mount. If he knows beforehand that these things don't hurt him, he won't be so upset when he sees me rise above him.

These are the steps in mounting the first two or three times. *Put just your toe in the stirrup. Always.* This is very important for safety because you want it to slip out of the stirrup if something spooks the

Saddling, Mounting, and Bitting

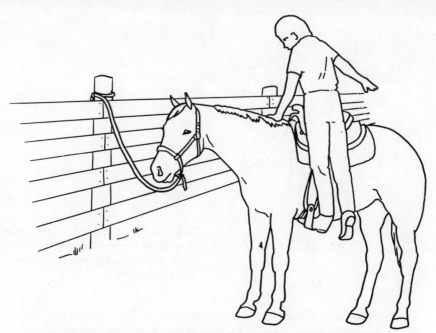

It is easy to stay balanced over the withers this way even if the colt moves around. Rub him all over and swing your arm over his rump so your leg coming over won't startle him.

horse. I never shove my foot home for mounting any horse. So with your toe in the stirrup, bounce up and down a few times. It takes a rather sudden upward push to get all the way up, and a few bounces will acquaint him with the possibility plus let him feel the cinch pinch.

Next, mount to where you are standing upright balanced over his withers. While in this position you can rub him on the off side front and rear, wave your right arm across his rump the way your foot will soon travel, and even rub him on top of his rump just in case you accidentally brush him with your foot as you finish mounting. If he should move around, you should have no trouble staying in this position.

The final step is to bring your right leg over and let yourself gently down into the saddle. I don't usually fish for that off stirrup right away even though my stirrups are set so it is easy to find. I just sit quietly and rub him on the neck on both sides. Then I gradually start moving around a little, put my foot in the stirrup, and rub my legs on his sides. Before I dismount, I remind him that the cinch will pinch by putting my weight in the near stirrup, and that my leg will swing across his rump by swinging my right arm there.

If the colt moves around when you are hopping up and down beside him, stop hopping briefly until he stands. Start the mounting when he is standing still, but don't stop or try to get him to stand the first several times during the mounting. Sometimes he has to move to catch his balance before he figures out what is going to happen and how to brace himself to compensate for it.

Let him move when you are on him if he chooses. If it is because of your movements, stop briefly and then try again. Don't try to teach him to stand still while you are on him. If you do this before you teach him to walk out, you can have trouble getting him to move at all when you first try. If you *start* each step of mounting when he is standing still, he will gradually learn to stand for the whole process without your having to teach him.

When I started Swede, I hadn't yet learned that many colts must move to catch their balance during mounting. I taught him to stand before I rode him and had great difficulty getting him to move at all. I still don't know if it was because I taught him to stand first or because he was afraid he would lose his balance with me on him. Strange as it may seem, some horses are afraid of losing their balance in what we would consider ordinary circumstances. I owned two horses, a mother and son, who were afraid of falling with one hind foot picked up. Horses may be big but balance is important to them.

You can either mount the colt the first two or three times you saddle him and then turn him loose in the corral saddled, or you can turn him loose saddled for one or two lessons and then mount him. If he seems rather tense about the saddle, you should do the latter. When you do mount him, get him used to it from both sides.

To turn him loose you need to bridle him with the snaffle bridle. If he is reluctant to open his mouth to take the bit, it is more effective to push your thumb up into the roof of his mouth than to press it down on his bars. Work slowly and carefully so you don't bump his teeth or pinch his ears.

The saddle must be cinched tight enough to stay in place. Ordinary tightness is sufficient unless your colt has very flat withers, in which case it does need to be a notch tighter. Make sure the bit is properly adjusted in his mouth, just barely wrinkling the corners. Tie the reins to the saddle so they are just loose when his head is at rest. This gives him a chance to get used to the feel of the bit in his mouth and to realize its limiting power when he lowers his head toward the ground.

I often tie the gunnysack to the back string of the saddle so it hangs down a ways, perhaps on the off side, and tie the coiled end of the lead rope to the near side so the end hangs down but doesn't drag on the ground. It isn't sensible to crowd him into panic by a rope dragging beside him even if he accepted it in sacking out. I continue that education when I have him and the rope under control when leading him.

To turn the colt loose, I lead him a few steps away from the tying post so he doesn't get the idea that he might be able to leave it on his own. This is one reason for having the tying post in the corral—you can lead him those few steps instead of farther, where he might spook

To bit the colt, tie the reins to the saddle so they are just loose when his head is at rest. Never try to set the horse's head.

out and break away from you. You should leave him loose for at least an hour, or as long as two or three. Just be sure to check up on him frequently.

There shouldn't be any projections in the corral to hang up the reins on, but colts can seem to invent ways to get in trouble. If you should have to help him out, approach his side deliberately as you tell him in a matter-of-fact tone of voice what a mess he got himself into. It will help keep him calm while you disentangle him. The truth is that I have never had one get in trouble turned loose this way in a *safe* corral, but I always check up often.

You should never shorten the reins to "set his head." A horse should walk freely forward toward the bit, not pull his nose back from it. He should develop the proper flexion at the poll over a long period of time because it should be the result of his accepting the bit more at the same time he balances more to the rear. A colt in his first year of training would carry his nose out somewhat if the training is proper. *So we do not set his head.*

There is one exception to the long reins during this get-acquainted-with-the-equipment period. Some colts will buck a time or two with the saddle bouncing in a trot or gallop and that is the end of it. A few will buck persistently. If the latter is occurring, get up to the colt and shorten the reins so they are quite snug but not pulling his nose in. Step out of the way and watch. When he tries to buck now, he will automatically bump his mouth with the bit and the timing will be perfect to discourage his bucking. When he settles down, go in and loosen the reins to the original adjustment. Two or three such sessions in that many lessons usually cure the bucking.

When it is time to end the lesson, take the lead rope loose and tie him up at his post. Remove the bridle very carefully by holding the crown in your right hand to hold the bit in position until he opens his mouth. Then you can carefully lower it. It helps to keep your left hand on his nose to keep his face vertical, if you don't try to use force. Just let him find out your left hand limits his movement, and proceed with the unbridling when he accepts that limitation.

Wiggle the saddle some before uncinching and removing it. A colt often forgets it is there and is quite startled when he sees it coming off his back. Brush him some to take care of the itchies and take him to his stall or corral. If you notice, you'll see in the way he walks that he is beginning to think he is "all grown up."

This whole lesson—refresher sacking out, saddling, mounting, bridling, and turning him loose in the corral—should be done for about three or four days, consecutively if possible. Then he should be ready for ground driving.

9
Ground Driving

Ground driving is a good educational step for the colt between mounting and riding. I always sack out and ground-drive a horse before I hitch him to a cart. To just hitch him up is sheer foolishness.

Between the mounting and the riding you can use longeing instead of ground driving, but it doesn't teach as much toward riding as the latter. Through longeing you can teach the colt to accept the bit and obey in walk, trot, canter, and stop. You can get him moving relaxed with rhythm and lengthened strides. But you can't teach him to do these things in response to the reins.

For longeing you need extra equipment—longe line, side reins, and a longe whip. Longeing is of no value if done improperly; in fact, it can even be harmful. The colt I mentioned that wouldn't stand for the saddle would also offer to bolt when being ridden. My friend said she always longed him first "to take the edge off."

When she stepped back and asked him to move off on the longe circle, he took off as if his tail were on fire. I immediately had her stop him and move closer to him for better control so she could keep him in the walk. I had her walk him both directions for a total of about fifteen minutes before I let her ease him into a trot. He wasn't learning anything except "Charge!" the way she was going about it.

It isn't easy to learn to longe a horse properly. You have to learn how to control him tactfully and use the whip, longe line, and your body language to get the proper responses. In *Everyday Training: Backyard Dressage,* I explain it all very thoroughly; so if you want to longe your horse, I suggest you get that book and study it and practice. In the meantime, ground driving will serve your present purpose much better.

When the colt shows he has accepted wearing the bit by no longer trying to spit it out, you can go on to ground driving. Control is essential so you should always have him tied to his post while rigging the lines. Control during initial driving is also very important, which is why I consider the fifty-foot corral essential. It limits his traveling area and also helps you teach him to turn and stop. A fence corner or the side of the barn can be helpful, but you still have wide open spaces where you can't keep up if the colt bolts.

The lines must be supported along the colt's sides at the girth area. You can use a surcingle with large side rings for this, but then the colt isn't getting used to the saddle creaking and flopping on his back. I use my stock saddle and run the lines through the stirrups. I don't hobble the stirrups because I want them to flop and pull out to the side for the colt to see. If his education up to this point has been correct, he won't be unduly startled by these things.

If I were using a flat saddle, I would hobble the stirrups because they are inclined to bang him on his sides instead of merely flop. Tie them together with baling twine or a small rope under his chest, leaving them loose enough to flop a little but not swing out more than six or eight inches. Secure the middle of this string to the middle of the girth so it won't slip back to pinch his belly.

You can also use single harness for ground driving. Don't use the breast collar and traces as they would just be a nuisance. If the harness has breeching, tie the holdback straps to the terrets to help hold it in place. Loosely hobble the shaft loops and run the lines through them. Do not run the lines through the terrets as it is almost impossible to control the green colt this way. Before he learns to respond to the lines, he can turn completely around to face you when they are run through the terrets.

Having the lines hang just above hock level gives you control of the colt's hindquarters, making it easier to keep him going ahead of you and to teach him what rein signals mean. It also controls his hindquarters to help him make his turns in a smooth arc, and this makes your work of teaching this under saddle a little easier.

With the colt saddled and bridled and tied to his post, tie the bridle reins to the saddle so there is a little droop when his head is at rest. Lay a driving line out behind you with no kinks or coils to get your foot caught in and thread the snap end through the stirrup from back

The colt rigged for ground driving in the harness—the holdback straps tied to the terrets to keep the breeching in place, the lines run through the shaft loops. You can't control him with the lines through the terrets.

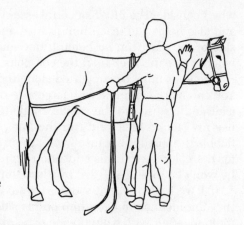

With both lines in one hand this way you can control the colt to pet him or adjust the equipment, whether you use harness or a saddle for ground driving.

to front and snap it into the bit ring. Lay the other line out the same way on the same side of the horse and put the snap end of it across the seat of the saddle. Go to the other side and thread it through the stirrup and snap it to the bit the same way.

Before starting to drive the colt, you should practice keeping him under control when you want to get up to his head out in the open. While he is still tied up, slip the off line over his hips, holding it so it contacts him just above his hock on the off side. This shouldn't bother him because of the sacking out you have done. The lines should still be laid out on the ground behind you on your right side and held one in each hand. Take short enough holds that you can take contact with his mouth without pulling on it.

As you move along his body toward his head, keep the off line just above his hocks as it comes around his haunches. Let it slip to maintain the contact without pulling. Shorten the near line to maintain contact there. When you are beside his shoulder, you can take both lines in either hand to maintain contact while you use the other hand to pet him or adjust the equipment. Of course, you reverse holds to do the same on the off side. With him tied up, practice this until you can do it easily.

To simplify the instructions on driving the colt I'm going to assume that you have the fifty-foot corral or a small fenced area at least thirty by forty feet. As I said in the beginning, that fifty-foot corral can be useful for many things and so is worth building. If you can't build it, renting the panels to put up a temporary corral is well worth considering for safety's sake. You would need it for only a month.

If you must use a larger area, make use of any barrier such as the side of the barn, a fence, or a fence corner where the area isn't cluttered with obstacles. Drive in forty- or fifty-foot circles so you are never far from the barrier.

If the colt does bolt when you are more in the open, immediately

drop one line and brace your hold on the other by leaning back on it.
This will turn the colt abruptly toward you, which is rather rough but
will quickly convince him he should not bolt. You can't hold him by
pulling on both lines. If you try to keep up with him, he will think you
are chasing him and run faster.

To start driving the colt, hold the lines in the control position I described while you untie the lead rope. Then step in back of the colt in
driving position between the lines, which should drag out behind you.
It is a good idea to stay about six or seven feet behind him for a while
just in case he does kick up even though this seldom happens. Maintain a feel of the colt's mouth through the lines without pulling on
them. You can get this feel through the weight of the lines. They need
not and should not be pulled taut.

Move him off by clucking and wiggling the lines. If necessary,
swing a line out and back in against his hind leg to get him to move.
Avoid pulling back on the line as you do this. If he is hard to get moving, you can carry a whip initially. Any slender stick about six feet long
will do. Tap him lightly on the side of his hip. If he doesn't move ahead,
tap him again a little harder, repeating until he does move. Be sure
you don't tighten the lines as he moves because that would send him
contradictory signals. As he moves off, walk with him. When he understands to go when you cluck or wiggle a line, you can dispense with
the whip.

The usual problem in starting the colt off is that he has only been
led up to now and so wants to come to you instead of walking away
from you. Almost always he will turn to the left to do this, so you need
to keep a firm contact on the right rein as he tries to turn back. It also
helps to position yourself a little to his right as the horse is less apt to
try to come to you on that side.

Always hold the lines so they contact the colt's hind legs just above
the hocks, as this helps control his hindquarters so you can prevent
his turning back. When he does walk away from you, make the contact
light and encourage him to walk on with vigor. You may need to start
over a few times, but with patience you can get him to understand
what you want. Don't pet him when he turns back, thinking to reassure him. He would think you approved of his reverse move.

Most people oversteer a green horse whether driving or riding, thus
pulling his head around while his body goes straight ahead. In ground
driving, the way to teach a horse to turn is to stop walking with the
turning hand fixed in place and the other hand yielded forward. Just
brace your elbow against your side as you move the other hand forward
an inch or so and stop (a brief hesitation), then take a step, stop, and
step until he does turn. Let your hands return to position to drive
straight on. Soon just bracing the turning line slightly back as you
yield the other one a little forward will turn him.

To ask the colt to halt, simply stop walking as you brace both arms against your sides. Say, "Ho, ho," letting your voice drop on the second ho, and stop. He will walk into the bit and stop—eventually. You may need to take intermittent steps forward initially to prevent his boring into the bit because he doesn't understand. When he does stop, relax your arms so the contact is immediately soft. If he offers to walk on, again fix your arms.

In turning and stopping the colt, don't try to force him by pulling back on the lines. What you are doing initially is explaining to him what you want by letting him run into the barrier of the fixed line or lines. After he understands, you continue the same tactics because it is more tactful. A horse that is taught to turn and stop this way will do so willingly without lugging on the bit. By his walking into the bit, he turns and stops himself. He hasn't been subjected to a force that will make him resistive.

In the round corral you won't need to do much steering initially because the fence will guide him around and around. In a square corral or approaching a fence corner, it is essential that you start indicating the turn before he gets to the corner. If he walks right into it, he will see a fence on each side of him and think he can't go forward; therefore, you should try to guide him past the corner so you don't have to start over by leading him out of it.

If you must drive through open area, you can help him make a circle initially by using slightly stronger contact on the inside line than on the outside. If you don't actually pull on the line, he won't resist it and you will gradually get back to your barriers. The time to start teaching him to turn is as soon as he shows he understands walking forward well. Start with gradual turns and advance to sharper ones as he shows understanding. Turn him in to make the circle smaller gradually and out to make it larger with simple, stronger contact on the one line. When he understands this, you can go on to real turns through your braced arm.

Then you can change the direction of the circle by turning across the middle and turning back the other way. Start the turn back the other way before you get to the middle because it will take him a few steps to respond. Don't feel you have to succeed on the first try and so force the issue. Just go on around and try again until both of you get the feel for it.

The purpose of ground driving is to teach the colt to walk forward relaxed and vigorously and to accept the snaffle in turning and stopping. This lays the foundation for the riding. There is one other basic you should teach him as soon as he is turning easily and that is to make a U-turn toward the fence to reverse directions.

Drive him parallel to the fence and about ten feet out from it. Turn him toward the fence the same way you make all turns, but yield more with the hand not turning him so he can make a shorter turn. When he is far enough around to see the fence with his other eye, yield with the turning hand to take off the pressure. He will finish the turn himself.

As the two of you get better at this U-turn, you can start him in it from about six feet away from the fence. It is important not to jerk him into the turn, so always bring your hand back smoothly as you stop dead still. It is important to yield the other hand far enough that the colt can make the turn and to yield the turning hand at the time he will finish turning on his own. And it is important to get him to walk out of the turn vigorously. This exercise prepares him for learning to double under saddle—a good safety and training maneuver.

When the colt is doing all these things well, he is ready to be ridden. The steps you have taken so far are sacking out, saddling, bitting, mounting, and ground driving. I continue to sack out a colt for about the first six days but not so thoroughly toward the end of that time. In saddling I continue to go through the tugging and wiggling process for two weeks or more. I go on mounting him each time before ground-driving him. He can be ground-driven before each riding lesson for as long as you feel it is necessary. All this routine is to reinforce his education through repetition.

There are more things you can teach him through ground driving, such as trotting on circles and through figure eights, turning on the haunches, side passing, and backing. In preparing the colt to be rid-

The U-turn, or double from the walk. Let the outside line slip so he can turn. At this point release the pull as he will complete the turn himself.

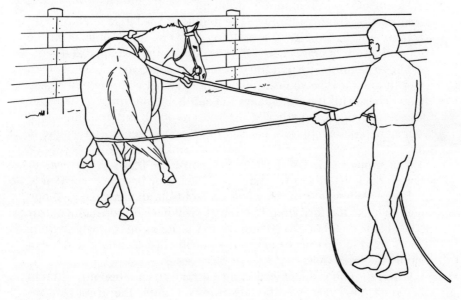

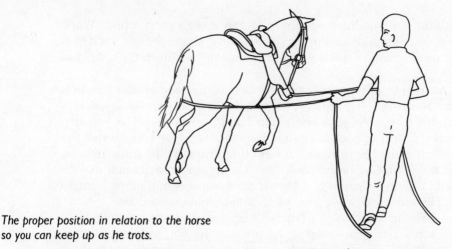

The proper position in relation to the horse
so you can keep up as he trots.

den, I don't recommend any of them except maybe the trotting on circles and through figure eights. Since I don't ask a colt to back until he readily yields to the bit and readily moves forward when I squeeze with my legs, I wouldn't teach him to back in the long lines. The other things are too confusing to the colt at this time, and he might use them against you when you start riding him.

It certainly isn't necessary to drive the colt in a trot, but you can choose to do it if you are able to handle the lines well. If you try to stay behind him in the trot, you invite disaster because you can't keep up with him. Using a shorter hold on the inside line and a longer one on the outside, walk on a smaller circle by staying even with his hips and about ten feet away. Be sure the colt is thoroughly obedient in go, turn, and stop before starting him in trotting.

In making the turn through the middle of the circle to change directions (the figure eight), everything happens much quicker in the trot, so be sure to practice first in the walk. As the colt approaches the middle to begin the turn in the opposite direction, you must take both lines in one hand so you can take a shorter hold with the new inside hand. Then with the lines again in each hand you must let the new outside one slip to lengthen it. As you are doing this you must take your new position opposite his other hip. So you see it isn't simple to do.

It is simpler to make the U-turn against the fence in the trot, although once again you will have to adjust your lines and position to make the complete turn. Stay out ten feet from the fence to give him room to make the turn from the trot. He will have to stop momentarily to be able to do it but can go into the trot again as he is finishing it. As I said, trotting isn't necessary, but you can choose to do it if you can handle the lines well.

When the colt is doing well in the corral, you can then drive him in the arena. This gives you the opportunity to guide him through a va-

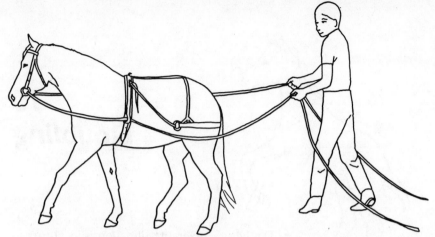

As you approach the center of a trot figure eight, you must take a shorter hold to turn the horse. Let the other line slip through your hand as you change sides behind him to take up the new trot position.

riety of maneuvers at the same time he is getting acquainted with the larger riding area.

You can get him going on long straight lines, in smaller circles, in half-circles away from the side to change directions, in crossing on the diagonals—whatever maneuvers you can devise that don't require sudden, sharp turns or stops. The only exception, of course, is the U-turn toward the fence, which is rather sudden.

Initially at the end of each driving lesson, drive him to his tying post to be tied up while you remove the equipment. As he gets more obedient, you can end the lesson at other places in the corral or arena.

Out in the open, snap a rope into the halter ring and drape it across your arm with no coils in it. This is not dangerous and you can quickly take hold of it if he decides to walk off. Almost always a colt is now willing to stand to have the tack removed. It is a good exercise for him to learn to stand quietly at more than one place, but it can't be expected of him at the beginning of a lesson this early in his training.

So in ground driving you have taught the colt to go forward and respond to the bit. You have avoided confrontation by letting him move into the bit instead of pulling on his mouth. You have reinforced these things and taught him obedience through careful repetition. There is just one more thing you need to know before you start riding him. That is how, when, and why to double him.

If you are starting a colt that you plan to drive, you should do all the training I have described up to this point. If he is to be solely a driving horse, you wouldn't have to mount him but it certainly wouldn't hurt to do so. When you reach this point in the indoctrination and training, it is time to introduce him to the cart. Turn to chapter 13 for instructions in this and his initial driving lessons.

Ground Driving

10
Doubling

Doubling—reversing direction in a U-turn— is both a safety device and a training device. It is often misunderstood, even by some who use it. Turning a colt in a short circle is not doubling him. Doubling a colt time and again against a fence may seem to "put a rein on him," but I have seen it done so excessively that you couldn't make a normal turn near a fence—the horse would swap ends at the merest suggestion of a turn.

When done properly, doubling gives you control of the colt under any explosive situation and also helps you train him to move forward well, to turn and stop well, and to start shifting his balance to his hindquarters. He must be schooled to double properly, not just hauled around so he sticks his nose up in the air and lugs on the bit. You can do this schooling in the fifty-foot corral or you can use the side of a building, high brush, or anything the colt will think he can't go over, under, or through.

Until a colt is predictably responsive to the reins, you should always ride with a shorter hold on the reins. Your hands will be farther forward than normal, but your elbows should still be bent to give you tactful feel of the colt's mouth and give your arms flexibility. There is no reason for you to carry your hands lower than on a level with your hipbones, but in teaching a colt to respond to the reins, you do lower your hands by opening your elbows. You should never lean over or entirely straighten your elbows in an effort to keep your hands low as this upsets your balance, which upsets the colt's balance. With the snaffle bit you almost never raise your hands to tighten the reins.

Maintaining a shorter hold on the reins makes it so you can respond quicker to a possibly bad situation. It makes it easier for you to double a horse before it is too late. For doubling it is also necessary that you can shorten one rein by taking both of them in one hand as you slide the other down the rein for a shorter hold. This is always the proper way to shorten your reins, first with one hand and then the other, so you should practice it until it is reflex action.

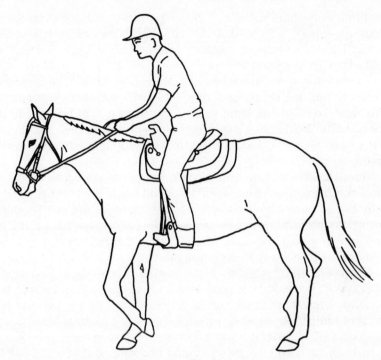

I use this forward position to relieve the colt's back in the trot—or you can post the trot. He needs to develop the use of his back before you sit the trot. Note this is not as forward as often used for jumping.

In riding the trot on a colt, you can either post or take the forward position. In posting, if you do it right by swinging your hips forward through your elbows as the horse pushes your seat up, you will never be more than an inch off the saddle. In taking the forward position properly, you will lower your knees toward the ground and bend forward from the hips. Instead of posting, you let your knees and ankles act as shock absorbers. Only your buttocks will come off the saddle

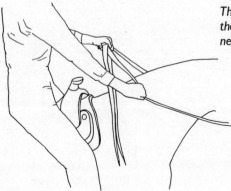

The proper way to take a shorter hold on the rein. You can do it very quickly when needed without losing control of the colt.

Doubling

and that only about an inch. This keeps you in balance even though your upper body is forward, and at all other times your body should be erect. These two relaxed positions are the most secure and save the colt's back from a pounding.

In doubling there are several things you must do almost simultaneously. You sink deeper into the saddle with your body upright. You take both reins in one hand to slide the turning hand down the rein for a shorter hold and at the same time bend the knee of the opposite leg to put your calf farther back to keep the colt's haunches from swinging out.

Immediately, as you give a series of boots with your legs, you smoothly bring the turning hand back and out into a very firm leading rein as you move the outside hand forward to let the colt be able to turn. The moment his outside eye sees the barrier, you release the pull and return your hands and leg to normal position as you give him another series of boots to keep him moving.

If you are riding a saddle horse as well as starting or planning to start a colt, it would be a good idea for you to practice the moves in doubling until they become reflex action. *Please do not use a curb bit for this.* Only in the most severe emergency is it permissible to pull on one rein with a curb bit. Only a thoroughly trained horse should wear a curb, so such an emergency should not arise. But you can use the snaffle and go slowly through the moves of doubling until you get them coordinated. Then you can practice to get the feel of actual doubling.

When you start the move to double the colt, you take his mind off whatever untoward thing he was thinking of doing. It is important that your pull on the leading rein be smooth, since jerking on it would cause him to put his nose up in the air and his mind on the pain in his mouth instead of on you. The barrier stops his notion of leaping

The start of the double against the fence. Make the pull smooth to avoid jerking, and keep your outside leg back to hold his haunches in place.

Starting the Colt

forward. When he sees the barrier with his other eye, he will finish the turn of his own accord, so it is important to stop pulling in order to enhance his response to the rein instead of just lugging on it. It is also important to move him out of the double because you want him to learn to go forward well and because a horse that is moving is less apt to pull a whing-ding.

In ground driving you have already laid the foundation for doubling and have probably even doubled him from the trot. Under saddle, start again in the walk about ten feet out from the fence and gradually get in to six feet from it. Keep him walking vigorously. When he is responding well from the walk, you can start doubling him in the trot.

You will notice that in the trot he must stop briefly as he makes the turn—his feet can't continue in trot sequence at the same time he turns right back on himself. Move him into the trot the moment his other eye sees the barrier. He will also make a very brief halt from the canter before he learns to roll back. Boot him into the canter as he is straightening out of the turn.

Doubling is the best way I know to prevent bucking and bolting. Notice that I said *prevent*. If a horse is already bucking or running, you can pull him down by trying to double him, so it is too late for doubling. The best thing to do then is try to boot him out of the bucking into running and slow down the running by turning him in a large circle that you gradually make smaller. Pulling on both reins to try to stop either bucking or a runaway is useless.

To prevent bucking or bolting you need to stay aware of the feel of the colt under you. For either one the colt will almost always slow down the briefest moment as he "squats"—brings his hindquarters under him. The vaqueros say he "grabs his tail." It is at this moment that you boot him ahead and double him practically at the same time if he

"Grabbing his tail." A colt will clamp his tail and squat before he bolts or bucks. He will slow down before he rears.

starts his head down to buck. Simply double him without the booting if he throws his head up to bolt.

Move him vigorously out of the turn, go a few strides and double back the other way, and continue with the riding that was just interrupted. You have taken his attention away from bucking or bolting and at the same time shown him he is to keep moving forward. It is difficult for him to move into either bucking or bolting without that little squat first. If he is just humping his back as if to buck or refusing to slow his speed so he might move into running, it is a good idea to double him. It will change his mind and make him more obedient.

A few colts may think about rearing. The best prevention is to move them forward vigorously, as they must stop in order to rear. You can safely do this because you can follow up with doubling if your thumping legs make the colt think of bucking or bolting. If a colt does manage to rear with you, lean forward and move your hands forward so you don't pull on his mouth and make him lose his balance. As his feet are coming down to the ground, move him forward quite definitely and double him if necessary.

When the colt has learned doubling in the small corral and been confirmed in it in the more open riding arena or area, you can then double him out in the open or against brush about the height of his withers. Just don't try it against a tree with branches he can duck under or you may find yourself doing an Absalom—hanging from a limb by your head. On a hillside, double him downhill so you don't pull him over backward. When it is the sort of hill you can ask him to climb, it is just as good to head him up it vigorously without doubling him.

Take care that you alternate sides in doubling as much as possible. This maneuver does help a horse learn to turn and you don't want him to get one-sided in his education. On the other hand, don't overdo the doubling, either in thinking to prevent improper moves on his part or to hasten his training. Most of the time just keeping a colt moving forward with vigor will keep him from thinking of bucking or bolting. As for hurry-up training, he has a lot to learn in carrying your weight over varied terrain, responding obediently and easily in the three gaits, and in stopping and turning. Don't try to hurry him out of kindergarten.

One other thing I want to talk to you about is tying the colt's head around. There are those who do this routinely before ever riding him. They recommend leaving the colt for an hour or much longer with his head tied to the rigging ring for the purpose of teaching him to turn or to "limber him up." Whatever reason they give, they are sadly mistaken.

The good western colt breakers never tied the colt's head around unless he absolutely refused to give to the bit to turn. When they did do it, they stayed right there until the colt made two or three circles freely and then took him loose. In my earlier training days I used it many times.

I remember one colt, a long-necked, lean fellow who could have his neck bent almost double and still run straight ahead. Even tying his head around didn't help. Now that I've learned more tactful use of the reins, I think I could teach that colt to turn. I doubt that I would ever have to tie a colt's head around again. One never knows, though.

In ground driving, the lines come to the bit at the level of the horse's mouth or lower. This encourages him to keep his nose down so he can respond better. If you handle the lines in stopping and turning as I described, so the colt goes up against the bit himself, you will almost never have trouble teaching him these things. The same is true if you will follow my instructions when you start riding him. So if the colt does bull on the reins during those first few rides, the first thing to do is to check up on what you are doing.

If you do have that rare colt that just doesn't want to respond by turning, first try stepping back near his haunches and taking smooth tugs on that one rein. By taking long, smooth tugs and being careful not to jerk, the chances are good that you can get him to take a step in your direction. Step up to his shoulder and pet him. Repeat the process several times and then try again, mounted.

If that process fails after several tries, then you can go ahead with tying his head around. It isn't a good idea to tie the rein to the rigging of the saddle. This is too solid, giving the colt little chance to escape the pull on his mouth. You can tie the rein to the stirrup. You will have to tie it almost next to the bit to get his head far enough around, but it can work because the weight of the stirrup puts moderate yet flexible pressure on the rein, thus coaxing him to turn. For this you use the slipknot.

The best way, however, is to tie to his tail. This gives the greatest

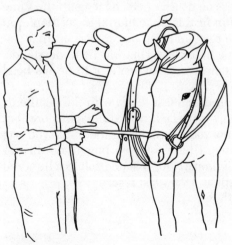

You can help him learn to turn his head to the pull of the rein while standing beside him. It is a good reminder if he bulls on the rein during riding.

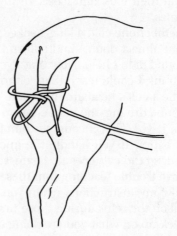

Tying the rein into the horse's tail with a loop for easy release. Tie the sheet bend just above the end of his tailbone and it will be just off the end when you pull it tight. (See the illustration on page 104 for the horse with his head tied around.)

flexibility without the weight on his mouth. At the end of the colt's tail bone, double the tail hairs around the rein. Gradually pull the rein through the doubled tail hairs to get the colt's nose almost even with the stirrup. If he starts moving in a circle as you do this, simply hold the rein in place in the tail and walk with him as he turns. If he doesn't stop, turn him loose while he is moving and pet him. After all, he's doing what you want.

If he just takes a step or two and stops, continue getting his head into position and then tie the rein to the tail hairs with a sheet bend and step back to let him figure it out. Usually the colt will start taking steps in a short circle very quickly. If he doesn't, encourage him to move by tapping him on his inside hip. When he has circled two or three times, step in to untie his head while he is moving.

If he is bulling to one side only, there is no need to tie his head around the other way. If one session doesn't help, do it again the same way. Never go off and leave him in this uncomfortable position. You are teaching him to turn to the rein, and it is very important that you reward him for turning by taking him loose. That way he understands. And no, you will not hurt his tail in any way using it to tie his head around.

This device should only be used as a last resort with the snaffle. It is used more frequently, but only if needed, with the hackamore. I'm sure that if you check up on how you are handling the reins, you will find the solution lies in that area. I have told you how to do this for two reasons: (1) so you can do it properly for that one colt in a hundred and (2) so you won't do it except as a very last resort.

11
First Rides

So far you have sacked out the colt daily to get him used to tack that can go slap and bump. You have saddled him, being sure he always sees what you are doing and being careful not to jerk the cinch up suddenly. You have mounted him from both sides daily and acquainted him with your movements in the saddle and the feel of its pinch and twist. You have turned the colt loose in the corral for a few lessons, saddled and bridled so he learns to accept them as harmless, everyday accoutrements. You have ground-driven him until he moves forward willingly, turns easily, and stops obediently. Now it is time to ride him.

During these first rides you will be teaching him to accept the feel of you on his back while he is in motion and to go, turn, stop, and yield to the bit. Because you are now on his back and the reins come to his mouth from a different angle, he doesn't automatically respond to them as he learned to do in the long lines. However, he will learn very quickly and continue in his established habit of obedience.

You will be teaching him to double and to carry you in the walk, trot, and canter. After the first lesson you will start teaching him to stand under saddle. If you consistently proceeded with each step of mounting only when he was standing still, he probably now stands for the whole sequence. If not, he soon will if you are consistent in going on to each step only when he is still.

When riding a colt you must always stay alert and relaxed. Yes, you can do both at the same time. You want to stay relaxed because the colt can feel you, and any tenseness on your part will make him apprehensive. You want to be aware of everything that is happening in and around the corral—a person or dog can suddenly appear—and of the feel and appearance of every move the colt makes. This way you can anticipate his moves so you can encourage the good ones and prevent the wrong ones.

On the day you plan to ride the colt, saddle him as usual. By now you probably just flop the saddle blankets on his back and go to the other side to pull them off and flop them in place again in the pretense that you didn't get them straight. You saddle him as a matter of course, being sure he is aware of all that you are doing and being careful to cinch up smoothly.

Ground-drive him through a short but thorough lesson, working out any mistakes he makes. When all goes well, stop him at his tying post to remove the lines and prepare to mount. With him untied and standing somewhat parallel to the fence, wiggle the saddle and check the cinch to show your intent and then mount in the manner that he has now accepted.

Remember to take up the reins before you mount. The near rein should be held short enough that you have contact with his mouth. With firm contact on the near rein and the off rein slightly loose, the colt will be inclined to turn toward you if he moves. This will prevent his escaping you and even help put you in the saddle if you are partway mounted. Put just your toe in the stirrup so your foot will slip out in an emergency. I mount all horses this way, not just colts.

Mounted, take up the reins in that shorter hold you must use when riding a colt and settle yourself in the saddle. If he starts to move off while you are doing this, let him. Otherwise, when you are ready, ask with a tap with your legs, repeating and making the tap stronger each time. If three or four taps don't move him, turn his head away from the fence with a leading rein as you tap him with your leg on the same side. This should get him off balance enough to start him moving. Be careful not to jerk back on the reins as you kick.

The moment he starts moving, relax your aids and apply them again only if necessary. Let him walk on and encourage him to do so with energy by staying relaxed in the waist so you go with his movement. At first don't try to guide him unless he is headed straight for the fence or into a corner. In these cases start coaxing him with the leading rein before he gets to the barriers. Those barriers can help him understand to turn.

For mounting, the near rein should be held snug but not tight enough to make the colt step back. It is wise to mount all horses this way—not just colts.

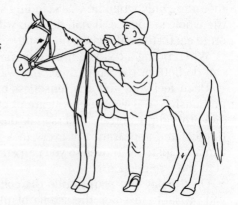

Starting the Colt

The main thing at first is for him to get the idea that he can move out freely with you on his back. If he breaks into a trot, let him. Usually a colt won't trot very far before coming back to the walk of his own accord, but once in a while a more nervous colt may start trotting faster and faster. If this seems to be getting out of hand, coax him to slow a little with smooth take and give on the reins just to keep him under control, not to slow him to a crawl.

If he doesn't respond to this, use the leading rein to coax him away from the fence and then double him into it. As his other eye sees the fence, release the pull and encourage him to trot on, repeating the whole doubling maneuver if necessary. It is better to trot him out of the double than to walk him because you don't want to discourage his willingness to move out. However, if he appears to be getting nervous instead of just too active, do walk him for a while until he calms down.

In all the times I've started colts, I can't recall ever having to double one on the first ride. You are asking nothing of him except to carry you around and to start responding just a little to the rein. All the groundwork has acquainted him with most of the flops and pinches that accompany being ridden so he doesn't get too concerned about them. If the colt is the more nervous type, you should do more ground-work before going on to the riding. But I do want you to understand that you can double a colt from a trot or canter in an emergency before you have gone through the steps of teaching him to double. That way you know you have a safety maneuver to use if he offers to buck or bolt when first ridden.

While it is okay to let the colt trot if he offers during this first ride, it isn't necessary to urge him to do so. Let him walk freely around the corral a lap or two and then start coaxing him to turn with the leading rein. If you have contact with his mouth with the turning rein, it tightens more as you move your hand out in the leading rein direction. The farther out your hand the stronger the "pull"; the closer in the less the pull.

So you can start your hand out and if he starts turning, you don't need to go farther. If he doesn't start turning, you can take your hand farther out but you must not just leave it there. You should move it an inch or so in and out so there isn't a steady pressure on his mouth. That way he will respond better.

Always move the opposite hand forward a little so the colt can turn his head to look where he is going. You look in the direction of the turn so your body takes the proper position for the turn. Always let your legs rest on the colt's body. Legs that stick out in front are useless. Legs that touch the horse only when asking him to move make him nervous. In the turns, bend your outside leg at the knee so it helps hold his haunches in place. Today you are starting to explain these aids to him. Use them.

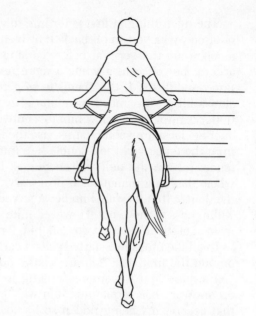

Using the fence to teach him to stop. Two slightly loose leading reins prevent his turning. Apply the stop signals a stride or two before he reaches the fence.

After several laps each way with the long gradual turns, you can ask the colt to come to a halt. Initially, you can avoid forcing him with the reins if you use the fence to help explain what you want. Head him straight toward the fence, stay relaxed down into the saddle, take a little stronger contact, and tighten and release over and over with flexible fingers—not with pull and push.

Start this a few strides before you reach the fence. He will stop when he gets there if not before. Release the contact and pet him the moment he does stop. When you don't pull hard to force him to stop, he will very soon relate your signals to the stop signals in ground driving. It is best not to make the stop at his tying post as that could make him head for it all the time hoping to stop, but it is a good place to stop if the colt is slow to understand.

Now it is time to start teaching him to yield to the bit when ridden. When you bitted him on the long rein loose in the corral, you let him learn for himself that the bit limited his reach. He lowered his head toward the ground, was stopped by the bit, and tucked his nose back. He yielded to it. When you drove him on the long lines and let him walk into the bit to turn and stop, he learned for himself the limits the bit imposed and he yielded to it. Now you are on his back and in a position to forget and pull on the reins. This can make the colt resist. Even if you don't pull on the reins, he can show some resistance, so you teach him to yield consistently. It is only when a horse yields that you have true control of him.

Each time you stop the colt you should then ask him to yield to the bit. Let him stand briefly to make sure he is relaxed. Take contact with

Starting the Colt

one rein without pulling on his mouth and brace that arm against your side so the contact stays steady. With your other hand use the leading rein to gently turn his head. If he tries to step back, close your legs a little on his sides and be more coaxing with the leading rein. Turn and slightly release his head with that leading rein over and over until he ducks his nose back. *Immediately release both hands and pet him.*

Don't try to force him to yield. If he is slow to respond, try reversing hands. Every horse has a "stiff" side and so will yield more readily on the other. After you get him to yield on both sides, give him a little more work on the difficult side to make it less resistive. When a horse yields to the bit, the contact feels lighter. It is very important that you release the reins the moment he yields. This rewards him for yielding. Trying to maintain the original feel of contact before he yielded punishes him for yielding.

It is better to turn his head against the opposite fixed rein than to tighten both reins straight back. He can resist the latter very easily. The former breaks the tension and gives his head nowhere to go but down and back.

Gradually it takes less leading rein and will work into your being able to tighten both reins straight back briefly to get that little tuck that says he has yielded. Do not try to make him carry his nose back this way or his face in the vertical. He is a colt and should travel with his nose a little forward in its natural position for quite some time.

Yielding to the bit is very important. You can't get any horse to do anything well if he won't yield. You can't control the colt with anything less than brute force if he won't yield to the bit. I never ask any horse for any performance before he has yielded, and in handling a colt this sometimes takes a lot of patience. When I want a turn or slowing or stopping or changing gaits up or down or any maneuver, I see first that the horse has yielded and then ask for what I want. Asking him to yield is saying "Please." When he yields, he is saying "I'm ready."

So in this first lesson get the colt to yield after the first stop. Then ride through several more laps and gradual turns each direction, stop him, and again get him to yield. Several times of this is probably enough for the first lesson and you can then dismount and put him away.

When I dismount a colt I'm riding, I first wiggle around some to be sure he remembers I am up there. Then I rise a little, putting my weight on the near stirrup to remind him how it feels. Then I dismount. Horses are very easy to get along with if you give them a chance to understand what is happening.

The second lesson should start out like the first with a little ground driving and then riding in a vigorous walk both ways and turns that gradually get sharper as the colt shows better understanding. Stop the colt several times, first headed toward the fence so it can help you and then beside the fence and eventually out in the middle. Ask him to yield after each stop.

Also ask him to stand briefly before moving him on. If he starts to move of his own accord, stop him and ask him to move only when he is truly standing still. Don't make a big to-do about it initially—just catch him in a moment of immobility to move him. If you are consistent in this, he will learn that he isn't to move until asked, and you can gradually get him to stand for longer periods of time. Do not try to back him. In about a month you will be able to do that simply by restricting him just enough with the reins that he won't move forward and closing your legs to tell him to move. He will then step back.

When he yields readily to the leading rein turning his head against the fixed rein, start asking for the yield by taking both reins straight back and up—these combined movements to be slight, tactful, and take and release over and over. When he yields, release completely. When he responds to this by yielding, you can ask this way as you ride along in the walk, being sure to close your legs on and off enough to keep him walking with vigor. You want him to understand that he is to keep moving, and you also want to push him into the bit to help him yield.

In between doing this work in the walk after the first several laps in both directions, you can urge him into the trot. Be sure your hands don't jerk his mouth as you trot him with vigor. Alternate a few times between walk and trot. Now you can start teaching him to double from the walk.

Staying out from the fence about ten feet to give him room to turn, keep him walking vigorously as you slide your hand down the rein to turn him directly into the fence with a low leading rein. As his other eye sees the fence, release the rein and urge him to walk on. Do this about twice each way so he understands what you are asking. Now

After learning to yield to the bit, the colt should tuck his nose to a brief take on the reins and squeeze with your legs in all gaits without slowing down. He doesn't keep it tucked at this stage of training.

Starting the Colt

Riding past the open gates of the corral and arena educates the colt to exit only when told to do so.

you can put him into the trot and double him twice each way from the trot. He will have to stop as he turns but can be booted into the trot as he is straightening out.

I don't often ask a colt to canter in the corral because of the limited space. Some horses naturally canter more than others, and such a colt might offer to do so. If he offers to canter that is fine, but be aware that this invites bucking in some colts. Coax him to stay a little away from the fence so you can double him if he offers to buck or bolt. Then move him on in the trot.

When he is doing well so you feel you can control him, it is time to ride out in the arena. Do this after warming him up in the corral in a review of everything you have taught him so far. When he has passed the review test, dismount and open the gate. Then mount up and ride him in the corral, passing the gate two or three times to show him that an open gate doesn't automatically mean exit.

This is an important part of his education. A horse that learns to bolt through an open gate can be dangerous. Such a horse threw me head first into the side of a tree trunk. If I had hit it squarely, I wouldn't be here to tell you about it. If I had been wearing a hard hat, I wouldn't have had such a headache. As soon as I have control of a colt, I teach him never to go through an open gate until I tell him, and I never ride any horse into a stall.

First Rides

If the corral doesn't open into the riding arena, it is better to lead him to that area initially. After passing the corral gate two or three times, ride through it, stop the colt, dismount, and take down the reins to lead him. Remember, you always want to be in position to control him, and he can easily jerk away if the reins are still on his neck.

In the arena walk him around once each way asking him two or three times to yield to the bit. Then urge him into the trot, initially following the fence and then going right on to other maneuvers such as large circles and changing direction by crossing on the diagonal. Arena riding should be a confirmation of his previous lessons, including doubling from the trot. You want to give him more room to move out and establish his obedience in the more open area.

It is also time to ask him to canter. At first follow the fence, staying out about six feet from it so you can double him if he gets overly enthusiastic and offers to buck or bolt. When he is cantering well, double him a couple of times going each way even if it hasn't been necessary. Boot him out of each double into the canter. You both need to understand the feel of doubling from the canter before going out on the trail.

I like to get a colt out on the trail as soon as possible and have found that two sessions in the arena are usually sufficient. However, none of this schedule I have laid out for you is written on tablets of stone. Some colts take longer than others—you have to use judgment.

It is better to err on the side of caution than to get in a hurry and come a cropper. I was helping a friend start an older mare. In my absence between lessons my friend said to herself, "This is too slow and rather silly. Why don't I just ride the mare."

The following day she confessed her impatience and the fact that the mare had bucked her off. Because of this incident it took us an extra two or three days to get the mare ready to be ridden. The moral: don't hurry up and have to wait.

12
Riding Out

Going out on trails is far better education for the green colt than working in the arena. In the arena you concentrate too much on teaching the colt various maneuvers that have no purpose in his mind. You expect too much of him and so push him too fast. It is necessary to devise exercises to help him develop his balance and carriage while performing with you on his back. These exercises do have some use later on in his training, but nothing can take the place of trail riding in a horse's education.

Out on the trail the colt sees a reason for tucking his hindquarters in going downhill, for gathering himself to hop over downed limbs, for maintaining his balance as he picks his way over uneven ground. You have a reason for turning him in going around brush or choosing a trail and so do it in a more relaxed and automatic way. In the arena we too often try too hard to apply the aids properly, get tense and out of position for what we are asking, thus making it difficult for the colt to understand and respond properly.

The very best trail riding is riding out on the ranch to check fences or cows that are due to calve or tagging along while others move cattle. In these situations you have a goal in mind and are more definite in a more relaxed way when asking the colt to go, turn, and stop. He feels your purposeful attitude and responds more readily.

But few of us have the opportunity to ride the range, so in riding the colt out on trails we have to define our goals in order to avoid either just going along as a passenger or pushing him to learn too much too quickly. You are out there to reinforce his obedience in the basic gaits and in turning and stopping. You want him to move freely forward where the trail permits and to carry you over a variety of uneven terrain in order to improve his physical ability and make future training easier for him and for you. You want him to learn to trust you so he will accept things that happen around him and the more difficult things you may ask him to do.

You have two things to consider before starting out. One is your

When riding out stay alert for things that go whoosh underfoot or crash through the brush.

colt's background. If he had a chance to run on hilly pasture with other horses, he will have valuable experience that makes your work less difficult. He has probably encountered the wildlife of the area—birds that fly up suddenly, deer that break out of the brush. He may even have had the opportunity to play in water. If he was raised in a small flat area, you will have to help him learn to go up and down hills and to accept weird-looking creatures that appear suddenly.

The other thing is his basic disposition. If he is a very calm colt, then he will probably accept different situations more readily, but you must not be lulled into thinking he will always respond like an old, trained horse. If he is a nervous colt, you must stay alert for what might crop up while remaining relaxed at all times.

Remember that you want to avoid confrontation that can lead to battles. You want the colt to enjoy learning all that you and the trails have to teach him. "No pain, no gain" does not apply to horse training. So each day you must choose which trail you will take to give the colt new experiences that start out easy, then gradually broaden into more difficult ones.

Another consideration in choosing the daily route is selecting terrain that can help you control the colt. The ideal in leaving home is a broad trail up a long, gradual hill. By the time you trot to the top, the colt is settled and ready to pay closer attention to you. Going downhill is harder for a horse and a colt is more likely to buck in that situation; therefore, a level trail is better than downhill, at first.

All horses like more open country better than wooded areas that limit their scope of vision. Calm colts will not be as upset by the latter as the more nervous ones. Brush scraping on your legs and the colt's sides can upset him as well as a tree branch rattling across your hat.

Starting the Colt

While you want him to get used to these things and should even go out of your way to let him experience them under controlled circumstances, you don't want to do it on the first two or three rides out.

An open field is better initially than a trail that is too difficult because of trees, brush, and uneven footing. In a large open field you can work the colt very much the way you did in the arena and go on a fifty-foot circle to control him if need be. You can also double him anywhere without getting into trouble. The open field and its environs may give you some hillocks, gullies, and brush to prepare him for traveling the more difficult trails.

It is wise to make use of the terrain in cantering the first few times. The best place is up a long, semisteep hill—one that will make him work a little but not make him lunge up it. There you can keep him headed uphill and not have to control his speed with the reins. If he offers to buck, urge him to put on more speed so he can't buck. When you feel him wanting to change to the trot, slow him into it and then into the walk.

Using the hill this way, you have taught him control without discouraging him and without a fight. If your only hill is the one near home, canter him up it at the end of your ride even if you are headed toward home. You can stop him before you reach home, turning him away to walk a distance before turning again to walk home. If you have only the open field, canter first on a large circle to help control him so you don't have to use the reins so much. When he will canter easily without wanting to buck or bolt, you can canter him other suitable places on the trail.

It is important when riding out to stay alert for possible surprises—alert but relaxed. I always watch for clumps of grass or brush that

Using a long gradual hill for introducing cantering on the trail lets you control the colt without pulling on the reins.

might harbor a pheasant, rabbit, or quail. I don't slow the colt down as that would make him nervous, but I'm ready so any sudden jump he might make won't unseat me and so I can double him if he decides to buck or bolt. A cow or deer in the brush can startle him, more so if it doesn't move because horses have a harder time identifying immobile objects.

By staying alert to such possibilities, you can avoid the embarrassment of being dumped and can calm the colt by closing your legs a little more firmly and talking in a matter-of-fact voice. One fellow came to me with the problem that his filly was bucking a lot. He had started her by just getting on and riding and had chosen to ride in a walnut grove. Any heavily treed area is a dangerous place to ride a colt. However, things went well until a pheasant suddenly flew up from under the filly's feet. She bucked, he fell off, and she continued to buck frequently on subsequent rides.

I've been caught a time or two myself when I failed to spot possible trouble. The most unusual time was when I was riding a filly in a large field of clump grass and small brush. It was toward the end of the ride and I was gawking at a hawk flying overhead when we were suddenly attacked from the rear. We had come too close to a hawk's nest and were being told in no uncertain terms to leave. Actually, the filly was

We can't anticipate every hazard out on the trail, but we can stay calm to help reassure the colt.

Starting the Colt

quite calm as I was the one under attack. I turned her sharply to the right and trotted away. Since then I've kept an eye out for aeries too.

Before you start out on the trail, go through a few warm-up exercises in the arena. Make sure the colt is yielding to the bit. Ride in all three gaits, making sure he will come down to the walk and halt easily. Do several turning exercises and double him at least once each direction. Then you can open the gate, remount, and ride him past it several times before going out.

The first couple of rides out should be over easy ground that offers no real difficulties. You just want the colt to see the country as you ask him to go through the things he has learned so far. I like to leave home in the trot because it is easier to control the horse in that gait than in the walk or canter.

Iam didn't cooperate in this on his first ride out. Because I live in flatlands, I hauled him to a park with hilly horse trails. Iam was corral raised and somewhat shy. There was no way he would trot up that first cut-bank road. He was sure there was a booger just around every curve ahead. However, walking him up the long grade was just as effective.

Two other corral-raised colts I started were just the opposite. Dos Reales would calmly and soberly go anywhere I pointed him. He had no fear of anything and no difficulty with any kind of terrain. This made his training much easier.

It was not the same with Ilak even though she was also unafraid. With her I had to keep telling her, "You can't go there." One time I had to stop her from walking off a five-foot sheer drop into a creek. I do think a horse should use a little judgment on his own, and I respect him if he is initially cautious. Boldness to the point of stupidity makes me nervous.

You will notice that most colts, unlike Dos and Ilak, on their first trips out look to you for protection. If you maintain a matter-of-fact attitude and select trails they can manage easily, they learn to trust you more. I generally try to keep a colt moving well where the traveling is easy, give him time to pick his way through if he is a little apprehensive, and give him experience in turning and stopping out on the trail.

From that time on I gradually introduce the colt to rocks and brush he must pick his way through, steeper hills to go up and down, water to cross, and so on. I always give him time to see what he must do to negotiate these things. If he acts as if he wants to lunge uphill, I stop him and let him look it over and settle down. Then I move him ahead in the walk, encouraging him with light contact on the reins since a big tug and release will only let him lunge ahead on release. If he has trouble going down hills, I support him with the reins with flexible

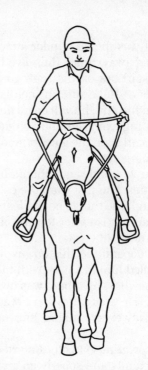

Framing. The two leading reins should just prevent his turning away, not hold him tightly in a vise.

fingers and help him tuck under behind by closing my legs on and off. I don't pull on the reins or kick him—I just support and coax.

A steep, short drop-off can make some colts balk since their eyes can't always judge depth. I use two leading reins loose enough that the colt can turn his head only two or three inches each way. This shows him he can't turn away but doesn't hold him in a vise. I close my legs a little more firmly to reassure him and give him a chance to look it over, even to lower his head if he chooses. When I feel him relax, I can then ask him to go on.

Sometimes it is necessary to lead him down. I like to carry my lass rope on the saddle when riding colts. In situations like this one I can put the loop around his neck, walk down ahead of him, and stay out of reach while I encourage him to lead down or across. Often a colt will leap such things instead of walking through, and the long rope lets me stay out of the way. A long lead rope will work as well.

After a colt has had several rides out, I also like to throw the lass rope out ahead of him and coil it up as we walk along in areas where there are no obstacles. I do this first in the arena and later in his trail riding after he has accepted many of the unexpected things we have encountered. Even though I can't rope anything, I feel it is good education for any horse to help him accept things you might want to do on or around him.

Some horses walk through water as a matter of course while others seem to avoid it like a Saturday bath. Usually you can feel as you approach the water if the colt is going to balk at it, but sometimes one will walk right up to the edge and suddenly put his head down and slam on the brakes. You can try framing him between the two leading reins to see if he will decide he can try wading in. I usually just dismount, take down the lead rope or put the lass rope on him, and wade into the water to play around, showing him it won't hurt him. He soon decides it's okay, and we wade around in it awhile before going on.

One thing you must not do is whip a colt to try to get him to go into water or up to anything he is scared of. He will think the scary thing is hurting him and be even more scared of it. You aren't spoiling him or teaching him to balk when you get off and go first to show him it's safe. You may have to lead him several times for the same thing, but gradually he will begin to trust you and let you ride him through the water or up to the scary thing. When the trust is built enough, you won't even have to lead him up to a new scary object.

I stay off car roads with a colt. Cars coming up behind him or head on toward him are monsters chasing him. The best place to acquaint a colt with traffic is in a field beside a busy road. There you can gradually get closer and plan it so you come in behind the vehicle so he can "chase" it.

You also can run into these monsters out on the trail. I listen for motorcycles and all terrain vehicles (ATVs) so I can find a place to get a few feet off the trail and ask the colt to stand facing it. Then as the roaring thing goes by, we fall in behind to "chase" it away—in a walk. Horses aren't afraid of things that run away from them. The first time I asked Iam to follow a motorcycle he tried to chase it in a fast trot!

Bicycles present a greater problem because you can't hear them coming and the horse is usually more frightened by them because they move without identifiable noise. I never ran into this problem when I was starting colts but if I did, I would ask the colt to stop and I would keep him facing the bikes by framing him with the two leading reins. I would certainly get the bikers to talk to me as that would help the colt identify them as people. If possible I would ask them to walk their bikes past us to help allay the colt's fear. If they are coming up from the rear, you should know it if you are alert to the colt's actions. Then you can turn him to face them.

Meeting other riders on the trail can cause problems. Here again I would stop and face them. I would explain to them that I am riding a colt and would they please proceed at a walk both approaching and until out of sight. If they want to stop and talk and my colt doesn't seem nervous about it, I would allow it briefly while insisting that a horse's length separate my colt from their horses. If my colt was nervous or excited, I would tell them it was nice meeting them but it would be better not to visit at this time. If my colt showed determination to follow them as they ride away, I would turn him in the opposite

If you must ride a colt on "civilized" trails, first educate him to bicycles and motorcycles in the arena.

direction to ride on. As his attention returned to me, I could then turn back to the way I was going.

It has been brought to my attention that many people don't have more isolated trails for riding. While I feel this is a distinct disadvantage because of so many potential distractions, it isn't necessarily a disaster. Most colts today are raised in the hubbub of civilization and accept that environment fairly well. Some of these are even quite nervous when first out in the wilderness.

Lack of such trails simply calls for more home education. Spend more time in the arena before venturing out. Get friends to help you by riding a bicycle and a motorcycle in the arena so you can follow them around, gradually getting closer and finally meeting them head-on. If you must then ride on more populated trails, a friend on a reliable, calm horse can be a big help to steady the colt's nerves. If you have nothing but car roads to ride beside, haul your colt to trails. It's cheaper than the injury a frightened colt can cause.

Another thing you sometimes have to teach a colt is to walk toward home. If you simply try to hold him to a walk, he can start learning to jig, which is very annoying. If you are in brushy country where he can go through the brush but not easily, you can just keep him in the brush and let him wear himself down until he is ready to walk. If you are in more open country, trot on a large circle until he shows he is relaxed. Ask him to walk and start toward home. If he won't walk, go on the circle the other direction. Stay with this until he is ready to walk home. Stay relaxed yourself and maintain walking rhythm in your body when you ask for the walk.

I got caught out once with no brush and no place I could ride the circle. Each time the colt went into the jig, I turned him in a very

Starting the Colt

short half circle—almost a double—and asked him to stand headed away from home. When he stood quietly, I turned for home. I had to repeat this several times, but he finally got the message and stayed in the walk. Whatever you do, don't try to hold him with a steady pull on the reins—that just supports him in the jig.

If you have a nervous colt, it is quite helpful to have a riding companion for the first few rides—*if the trained horse is quiet and obedient and the rider knows that what his horse does influences what the colt does*. Your companion should stay alert to how your colt is behaving so he can put his horse in a position to reassure the colt if needed. He definitely should not just take off down the trail without looking back.

Another reason to have a companion along is to deal with the possibility of the unexpected. My friend Mary got in a bind with her filly. She and her friend rode across a meat bee nest. The meat bees, or yellow jackets as they're called in California, nest in the ground and there's no way you can spot the nest. Those bees swarmed Mary's filly, stinging both of them repeatedly. The filly bucked Mary off and she fell on a rock, bruising her kidney, which was very painful. Her companion was there to help her get back to the trailer, load the filly, and drive them home. I should again advise you to wear a hard hat. Others have landed on their heads without the hard hat—some with serious results.

While it is better not to ride alone, I prefer to because it is easier to keep the colt's attention on me and what I'm teaching him. Riding with someone makes it too easy to fall into the trap of just going along for the ride. If you do go with someone, you must concentrate on taking the lead sometimes, turning off to make detours away from the other horse at times—little things that make the colt obedient to you instead of just a tagalong. After the trained horse has shown the colt that water or other boogers are safe, you should ask your colt to be the first to go through or up to them.

Riding out on the trail reinforces the basics you are teaching the colt and gives him experience in all sorts of situations. You should make sure those experiences start out easy and gradually get harder. You should soon teach him to stand patiently both under saddle and while being mounted out away from home. Hill country will develop his muscles and balance far better than arena riding and won't bore either of you into rebellion.

I like to take occasional long rides on the colt, packing a lunch for both of us. We explore country new to him. He learns to relax tied up away from home, and the greater distance tires him just enough that he settles down to acting more like an experienced saddle horse. After about a week of trail riding of an hour or so each day, the colt is ready for a three-hour ride with a lunch break. A friend who started many colts told me she always packed a sandwich when riding them out. When she started to lose her temper, stopping to eat the sandwich calmed her down.

After a month of trail riding the colt is ready to move into more serious training if he is at least three years old. If he isn't three yet, you can turn him out for the winter to run with other horses. In the spring, before starting his basic training, give him a brief refresher course. If you can't turn him out, continue to trail ride once or twice a week. It will help prepare him for further training later.

My book *Everyday Training: Backyard Dressage* explains in detail the way to train a horse in his foundation education and how to apply that training to specialties. The solutions to any problems you encounter are covered in *There Are No Problem Horses—Only Problem Riders*.

Remember to avoid confrontation in starting the colt and in all training. Give the horse time to understand, time to respond, and time to get in the habit.

13
Driving to the Cart

I select driving horses carefully because there are more possibilities for trouble in driving. I want a calm, steady horse that doesn't shy suddenly or persistently. It is harder to get a nervous horse to accept the weird noises a cart makes chasing him down the road. A horse that shies a lot probably has defective eyesight and so could not be trained out of it.

I also am particular about equipment. It may be true that blinders will prevent shying, but I never use a blind bridle on a harness horse. An old-timer who had earned a living breaking team horses told me that more accidents were caused by blinders than by anything else. The team is standing there dozing and the farmer throws a plowshare in the wagon with a big clunk. The horses spring awake, think something is attacking from the rear, and take off like a landslide.

Many things can startle a horse who can't see all around him, yet the stupid show rules won't let you show a horse in an open-face bridle. But then there are quite a number of horse show rules I disapprove of, one of them being not letting you show a trained saddle horse in a snaffle bit.

If you think you must use a blind bridle, make sure the blinders stand out from the horse's eyes. That same old-timer said they should be almost at right angles to the horse's head. You don't want the horse to have only tunnel vision. If I were going to use a blind bridle, I would train the horse first with the open-face bridle.

The other thing I don't approve of is the overcheck. I always rig my driving bridle with a sidecheck, which is far easier on the horse's mouth. Either one should be adjusted so the horse can lower his head at least to level. A horse that must pull heavy loads needs to get his head even lower. The only acceptable purpose of either check is to keep him from getting his head so far down that the lines can get tangled. Using either one to keep the horse's head high is not only vanity and cruelty but stupid because you want a driving horse to yield to the bit the same as a saddle horse. He can't do it with his nose in the air like a snob.

Show harness often has cups to fit over the ends of the shafts instead of breeching. I suppose this is okay for horses that don't really do any work, but it puts the load of stopping, backing, and holding back going downhill on the saddle, bellyband, and crupper and so on the horse's girth and tail. If you are going to have him pull any kind of load at all or use him on hilly roads, you should use breeching harness. That way the horse's haunches do the work of holding back or pushing back the load.

One other thing on equipment. Most of the modern carts I've seen don't have singletrees. Instead there is a hook on each side of the frame to hook the traces on. Those traces are attached to the breast collar that comes across the horse's shoulders, which work back and forth as the horse walks and trots. The singletree is there to swing with this motion so the horse doesn't wear sores under the breast collar. If your cart doesn't have a singletree, it is very easy to make and install one or have your blacksmith do it. See the diagram and instructions on page 83.

There are some important things in harnessing. The positions of the breast collar and breeching should be such as to make the horse's work easier. The breast collar should hang at the junction of the horse's neck with his breast. The breeching should hang on a level with his stifles. The crupper should be adjusted so it stays in the groove at the horse's dock, but it should not be pulled tight because that would make it rub a sore.

I like the crupper that has the buckles for additional adjustment and for opening to put it under the tail. Whichever kind you have, always lift the horse's tail to position the crupper and pull all the hairs out from under it. Always lift his tail to remove the crupper—never, never just jerk it off. Cinch up the bellyband smoothly and by degrees. The adjustment is the same for harness and saddles.

Every colt that is to be driven to a cart or other vehicle should be sacked out thoroughly, bitted, and ground-driven until he is completely obedient to the lines. In sacking out he should definitely become acquainted with the feel of the stick and the rope under his tail, not just in the groove at the dock but farther down too. Many a horse not indoctrinated in this has run away when he got his tail over the line and clamped down on it. The driver is helpless to control him in this situation.

It doesn't hurt anything to mount the colt in the course of this preliminary education even if you don't intend to ride him later on. Just being driven doesn't ensure that a horse will accept being ridden. Midnight, one of the most famous early-day bucking horses, was a gentle buggy horse until someone tried to ride him. He bucked with such

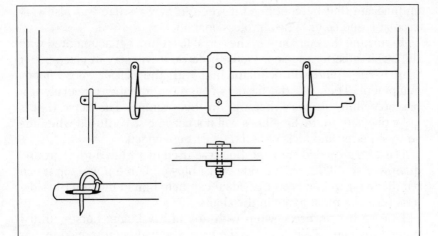

The Singletree for a Horse Cart
Materials

¾" galvanized pipe 30" long or 2" shorter than the distance between the
    shafts at the frame, whichever is less
Two steel plates 1½" × 4", ³/₁₆" thick
Two ⁵/₁₆" bolts 2½" long with 2 nuts each
Two ³/₁₆" bolts 2" long with 2 flat washers and 1 locknut each
Two ¾" leather straps 10" long
Two pieces of leather bootlace 7" long

Flatten the ends of the singletree about ¾" and cut out the fronts of the
flattened ends to fit the slots in the traces. Drill an ⅛" hole in each end on the
outside of the traces.

Drill matching holes ¹/₆₄ over ⁵/₁₆" in the 2 plates, centered ½" from each end
and in the centers of the frame and the singletree. Bolt the plates on either side
of the frame and the singletree. Double nut the bolts to secure them but let the
plates and singletree swing.

About 8 or 9 inches out from the center on each side drill a ³/₁₆" hole (top to
bottom) in the frame. The leather straps are bolted on here (the ends on the top
and bottom of the frame) to go around the singletree just loose enough that the
ends of the singletree can swing about an inch forward and back. Try it to see
where to punch the holes in the straps. Bolt them on with a washer on each side
and secure with the locknut.

Cut a slit in one end of each leather shoelace piece. Fasten them around the
tops of the trace slots by pulling the ends of the thongs through the slits. When
the traces are on the singletree, each thong is slipped through the holes at the
end to keep the traces from slipping off.

This installation should be strong enough for a horse to pull two people in a
cart. For a pony cart the singletree is 26" long. My measurements assume the
frame of the cart is ¾" pipe.

enthusiasm that he continued it when in harness. He was also very good at it and so became a professional bucker.

In turning the colt loose in the corral to let him get acquainted with the bit, it is better to use a saddle because it will stay in place better than harness and will acquaint him with the noisier, more floppy equipment. Then use the harness for ground driving, especially if it has breeching. Be very thorough in this training. The horse that is quite obedient in the long lines will not become so confused when the strange noises and feels of pulling a cart are added.

It is also a good idea to get the horse used to a whip during ground driving. Use it both on the side of his hips and on top. On top it can tell the horse to move; on the side it can help him in making the side-pass turns he must make in the shafts.

I never had to use a whip with any of my buggy horses until I trained my pony, Pepperoni, to the cart. She had been spoiled by her youthful owners into believing she could always get her own way by balking, kicking up, or rearing. In ground-driving her I had to hit her two separate times for each one of these breaches of etiquette. Then I always carried the whip to remind her to behave. I also found it useful in some of her training.

If this is your saddle horse you have decided to drive, do get him used to the stick and rope under his tail and thoroughly obedient to ground driving. Follow all procedures in hooking him up as if he were a colt. Just because he is an obedient saddle horse, don't think he will automatically accept the breeching and the cart and their feels and noises.

If you are starting two horses to drive as a team, first train them to drive separately to avoid a chain reaction if something goes wrong. On the other hand, hooking up a colt with a trained harness horse can help him learn. He still needs the preliminary work first, however.

During the ground driving I like to have the cart where I can lead the colt up to it to let him see and smell it. Then in arena lessons I like to drive him past it several times each lesson and even up to it to stop and stand briefly. If you have a helper, it is a good idea to have him pull the cart ahead of the colt as you ground-drive him and then behind him and you. A horse isn't afraid of anything going away from him and will subsequently accept the sight and sound of the cart behind him.

I never liked the idea of backing a horse between the shafts to get him in position to be hooked up. It looks awkward and silly, especially if he is wearing blinders and so can't see behind him. The other thing is that I almost always work alone, and positioning him this way would mean that I would have to hook him up without having absolute control of him.

I always tie the colt to a hitching rail or other good tying place where

I prefer to bring the cart to the horse. If he's well sacked out, he shouldn't object. See the text for one that did.

there is room to turn him away from it after he is hooked up. Then I bring the cart up behind him with the shafts raised to position it and lower the shafts in place. I never had this bother any horse until it was time to hook up Pepperoni.

Pepperoni was completely complacent about sacking out and being ground-driven. She walked up to the cart readily. Yet those shafts raised and coming up behind her freaked her out. I always blamed it on the bright yellow I had painted the cart. I know they say horses are color-blind, but there is an abundance of evidence that they recognize light intensity, which is one aspect of color.

Regardless of the reason for her fear, I had a problem to solve. More sacking out and more visits with the cart and trying to bring it along her side didn't help. So I simply got between the shafts myself so I could lead her beside the cart. It took several days working both sides of her before she finally accepted it and was broke to pull the cart. Always when you run into a problem, it is wise to stop and think it through and then proceed cautiously with each idea until you find the one that works.

There are those who use a kicking strap when first driving a colt. This is a strap that attaches to the harness on top of the hips and then to the shafts on each side. Supposedly this prevents the colt from kicking up high. I have never used a kicking strap or had any need for it. The preliminary work takes most of the startle out of being driven. Only once did a colt even offer to kick up. She was a bit startled at the feel of the breeching tightening when she first went into the trot. She

Driving to the Cart

humped into a little kick and I asked her to walk. Then I put her into the trot again and she accepted it like a pro.

There are safety rules to follow in hooking up a horse at any time. If you lead or drive him to the tying place after he is harnessed, lay the traces across his back. You don't want them dragging for him to step on, and you do want them handy to take down to hook up.

If you lead him to the tying place, the first thing to do after tying him up is to run the lines through the terrets, attach them to the bit, and lay them out on the ground on the near side. They will be within reach on his back from either side. There may be no chance that he can get loose, but this is an essential habit if later on you hook him up without tying him.

After running the shafts into the shaft loops, always hook up the traces first and take them loose last before backing the cart out of the loops. If a horse takes off only partly hooked up, it is safest if it is the traces that are attached. With a pony it is very easy to reach across and hook the off trace first and then the near trace. It could be possible to do it with a horse so you don't have to go around leaving only one trace hooked up.

Next come the tiedowns at the shaft loops. Adjust these so there are three inches or so of up-and-down play in the shafts. They just keep the shafts from raising up too high when going downhill or backing up.

Finally, I wrap the holdback straps. Bring these straps under the traces to help hold those up. After taking the wraps on the shafts, you can buckle the end either under or on top of the trace. Just don't take the wraps around the trace as well as the shaft, as it needs to have freedom of movement. Hook up the sidecheck or overcheck just before moving off, and unhook it the first thing when you are through driving. Unhitch in the reverse order.

The holdback strap in place so it helps support the trace without restricting its movement.

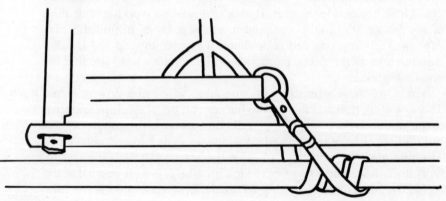

Starting the Colt

There is an important thing about the adjustment of the shafts. They should hang just above or just below the point of the horse's shoulder. I had trouble getting Pepperoni to make the side-pass turn from the standstill until I realized the shafts were contacting the point of her shoulder as she turned. I raised them an inch and immediately she side-passed like an old experienced buggy horse.

The first few times I hook up a horse I take plenty of time checking out all the adjustments, wiggling things here and there, and talking things over in a matter-of-fact tone of voice. When everything is adjusted properly, I then push and pull the cart several times to let the horse experience the feel of the breast collar and breeching tightening on him.

Now I take up the lines so they won't be hanging and dragging as I stand by his head and untie him. The next step is tricky because I must coax him to turn away from the tying place. As he tries to turn, he contacts the near shaft and naturally thinks it is a barrier. I help him by pulling the shaft toward me as I lead him to turn. Invariably we proceed one step at a time to help him through his confusion and to avoid panic. Soon I have him lined out in the clear where he can safely pull the cart away.

Initially, I lead the horse until I see he is accepting the cart. Then I position myself beside his hips to drive him from there. This gives me better control if he is a little spooky and psychologically keeps me talking in a calm voice. From this position I can drive him on the straight and in wide turns. At each practice stop I go to his head to help him make a short turn so he can learn the feel of contacting the shafts and how to side-pass instead of trying to turn his body in a circle.

The next step is to drive from farther back and eventually from behind the cart. Of course, you can't do this with a buggy so you just have to be thorough in driving from beside the horse until you are sure he has accepted the vehicle behind him and is obedient in go, wide turns, and stops. Then you can get in the buggy.

With my cart I can sit sideways on the seat at the rear as we drive along, and when I see that all is going well, I then turn around so I am completely in the cart. I may seem overly cautious, but my main concern is to avoid any accident that will make the training harder or even ruin the colt for life as a driving horse.

I can usually do all of these things and even trot the colt in the first driving lesson. You must use judgment in this, proceeding at the colt's rate of acceptance. Half an hour of driving is ample for the first lesson or two. The short lessons will avoid numbing his brain, and the long rest between them will give him time to absorb what he has learned.

Right here I want to talk about contact with the horse's mouth through the lines. People who want a stylish driving horse are inclined to take too strong a contact. The lines can have a slight sag at the bit and you will still have contact (feel) with the horse's mouth. An obedient horse doesn't need more. You handle the lines the same as in riding—with flexible fingers and movement of your arms from the shoulders. Your elbows should be bent. I've seen many people nowadays driving with their arms straight, their hands far in front of them. This creates tension, which makes tactful use of the lines impossible. It is very unprofessional.

A horse that has a high threshold of pain will take stronger contact on the bit. If you are tactful and consistent in his obedience lessons, the contact will get lighter as the horse improves in performance—*if you let the contact stay light each time he makes it light.*

A horse that has a very sensitive mouth is more difficult to train whether it is in riding or driving. It is very difficult to use the reins or lines gently enough that the horse doesn't overrespond to them or even get upset and rebellious at the pain. Instead of bragging about your horse's sensitive mouth, get a bit with a rubber-covered mouthpiece so you aren't hurting him. His performance will improve greatly.

Pepperoni was such a pony. I couldn't drive her in a straight line because of this. Not wanting to invest in another pony bit, I wrapped each side of the mouthpiece with strips of denim from old jeans, tying them on with cotton string. Immediately I could drive her straight and make smoother turns and found her more obedient than before. I could replace the denim any time it got dirty. I did find that it was better to dip the bit in water just before putting it in her mouth as the denim would harden some from her saliva, even though I rinsed it off after each use.

From this point on you want to build the horse's performance step by step. You want him to walk and trot with vigor; to change gaits and stop readily; to stand while you get in and out of the cart and for brief periods during driving; to wait for your signal before moving on; to make wide, smooth turns and side-pass turns from the halt; and to back readily.

It is helpful to use the whip on top of his hips, if needed, to encourage him to move readily and on command. In asking him to stand, don't try to hold him with a steady pull on the lines. The same is true in asking him to change from trot to walk to halt. Take a little firmer contact and ask him down with squeeze and release over and over with your fingers. Ask him to stay standing the same way. In all these things you must give him time to respond at first and build it into ready obedience through repetition, consistently using the same signals.

In teaching him to stand while you get in and out of the cart, pay attention to his body language. Patiently wait for him to relax in standing, then get in or out while maintaining contact that lets you tactfully signal him to stop if he starts to move. Don't let him move off imme-

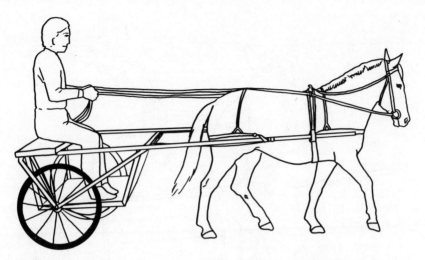

A willing colt with everything in place. I never needed a whip with any of my driving horses until I trained spoiled Pepperoni. It can be useful in training.

diately after you get out or after you get in until you are settled and ready to drive. Eventually he will associate your getting in and out with standing and do so.

Turns in motion, at first wide and gradually sharper, are made more smoothly if you maintain a light contact with both lines. Yield the outside hand enough, without losing contact, that the horse can make the turn. I eventually trotted Pepperoni through figure eights. You must be sure to allow enough room for this maneuver because you can't ask a horse to turn sharply in the trot.

Turns from the halt are more advanced and can be started after about a week of driving. Up until the time you think the horse is ready, get out of the cart and lead him through such turns in both directions. In leading him away from the tying place, alternate between sides each day, in addition to leading him in a turn or two each way during the lesson.

In order to turn a horse that is standing still, you must take firm contact with both lines and then through squeeze and release over and over with the turning hand coax him to side-pass to make the turn. You can see that this can be confusing to the colt, and it requires good response to the lines. Gently tap the horse on the outside of his hip with the whip to help him move his hindquarters. If he has learned the maneuver well when you led him through it, he should be able to understand the lines and the whip and will turn when you are in the cart.

If he still has trouble with it when you are driving or has trouble learning to sidestep when you lead him in the turn, you can help him with a few ground lessons. In between driving lessons, halter the

Driving to the Cart

In the standing turn the colt initially tries to turn instead of sidepass. A tap with the whip on the outside thigh helps him move his haunches over.

horse and lead him to a smooth area and ask him to stand. As you barely turn his head toward you and softly restrain him from stepping forward, tap him on the side of his hips with a short whip. The moment he takes a step with a hind foot away from the whip, remove it and release his head and pet him.

Repeat this two or three times on that side and then go to the other side to get the same results there. It is better then to stop the lesson and give him another later the same day or the next day. When he is making this turn on the forehand easily, you can then turn his head slightly away from you and coax him to step away from you and the whip both front and rear. This side pass will be wiggly at first but gradually get smoother. These exercises not only help him understand that you want the side pass in the standing turn but also help him develop the physical ability to do it. He will also understand the whip signal on the side of his hip better.

You can lay the foundation for backing in the cart when doing the ground driving. Either there or in the cart it is much easier to teach him to back if he accepts the tap of the whip on top of his hips to move

Starting the Colt

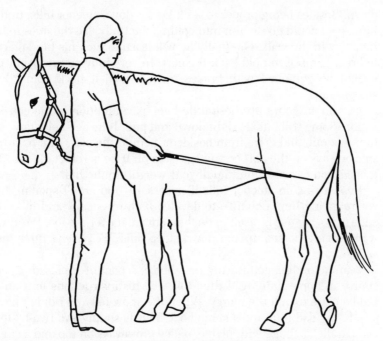

Start with the turn on the forehand like this. Then you can get the side pass by turning his head slightly away as you tap with the whip. Then you can get the standing turn in the cart.

forward. Without that both in ground driving and in the cart you must be very tactful with your hands to get him to take a step back rather than forcing him to back with a strong pull on the lines.

It is so much better to get the horse responding to the whip on his hips to move forward readily. Then when he has accepted the contact on the bit, it is simple to back him. Take a firm contact that softly tells him not to move forward, and then tap him gently on top of his hips. He will step back. This takes some experimenting to get just the right amount of contact without pulling on his mouth and the right amount of whip to avoid confusing him.

This is how I asked Pepperoni to back with the cart—with the firm contact and the whip. The first few times I did it when I was out of the cart so she wouldn't have to push a load backward. When she understood and backed readily, I then stayed in the cart. There was never any trouble. This brings me to another very important point.

Be very careful in how much load you ask a horse to pull initially. The surest way to make a balker is to ask him to pull a heavy load before he has learned to pull the cart easily and has been built up physically by gradually increasing the type and amount of work.

The colt's first driving lessons should be on flat ground. After a few days of driving, you can go down and up short gradual hills. Walk him down. Besides being proper to walk horses down steeper hills, trotting him down could goose him into bolting. Tactfully use the lines to help him stay in the walk. Gradually he will learn to tuck his hindquarters to brace himself to hold back the cart. In very hilly country your cart should be equipped with brakes to help hold it back going down steeper hills.

Initially in going up these little hills, pay attention to the colt's reaction. Some will buckle right down and pull. If he acts reluctant, stop him, get out, and drive from beside or behind the cart. The next time sit sideways on the cart so you can step off if he is reluctant. In a few lessons you can ask him to pull your weight up the hill.

Repeat this on steeper hills if necessary. You aren't spoiling him; you're giving him a chance to develop both physically and in knowledge of how to use himself to the best advantage for the job. We always walk driving horses up and down steep hills. *We never canter them, ever.*

Years ago after getting my first horse, I bought Professor Beery's course in horse training. I then followed his instructions to train my saddle mare to pull the buggy. When the snow fell and I didn't have a sleigh, my dad built me a stone boat. This is simply two two-by-fours laid parallel on edge with planks nailed crossways on top and a single-tree attached at the front. Back East they were used to haul boulders out of the fields, hence the name. My mare and I enjoyed our "sleigh rides" and I used the stone boat to haul baled hay home from where I had it stored four blocks away. When the snow melted, she leaned into the collar to pull the load over the bare pavement. I was very proud of that mare. Because I built up her loads gradually, she was very willing to work hard when asked.

There was another interesting development in driving Pepperoni. After several lessons, I wondered why she sometimes stood while I got in the cart and other times tried to start off. In reminiscing about Professor Beery and his methods, I found the answer.

Professor Beery went from town to town curing outlaw horses of their bad habits. It was somewhat like a circus. People paid him to cure the horses, and many more people paid to get in the tent to see him do it. To advertise these sessions, Professor Beery drove a span of light horses through the town with no bridles on them. He controlled them with whip signals.

Aha! I realized that sometimes when I got in the cart I held the whip down and at other times up in the position I held it during driving. Without realizing it I had taught Pepperoni whip signals during driving that told her to go and stop. From then on I was careful to keep them straight so I wouldn't wrongfully accuse her of disobedience. Horses can be quite amazing.

Starting the Colt

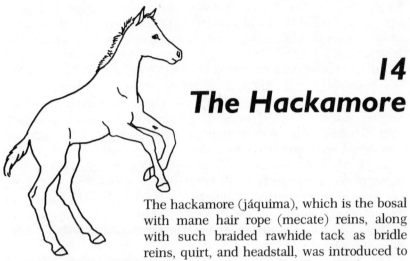

14
The Hackamore

The hackamore (jáquima), which is the bosal with mane hair rope (mecate) reins, along with such braided rawhide tack as bridle reins, quirt, and headstall, was introduced to Spain and Portugal with the invasion of the Moors.

History tells us that the Moors were able to conquer the Iberian Peninsula because of the agility and training of their horses. The heavier Spanish horses were trained to carry their armored riders in headlong charges, while the Arab-blooded horses of the Moors could easily outmaneuver them with sharp turns, quick stops, and sudden leaps into action. The Andalusian and Lippizzan horses and the training of them stem from the barb horses and the training the Moors gave them. Portuguese bullfights are performed by horsemen. There you can see the sort of training the barb horses were given.

We know that the Spanish settled much of the Americas. What isn't so widely known is that much of California from Tejon Pass northward was settled by Portuguese soldiers of fortune who were given Spanish land grants as payment for their military services to Spain. All systems change in various ways through use by different peoples in different circumstances. The Spanish Riding School in Vienna and the California reined stock horse perform the same maneuvers but in different ways. They come from the same source—the Moors.

The hackamore is used in South America, Mexico, and north through Arizona, California, and Nevada into Oregon, Idaho, and Montana. The ways these people use the hackamore are rather varied, and even in California there was a difference in application north and south of the Tejon Pass. The Portuguese horsemen were more dedicated to the understanding of horses in their training, and so their methods were not so severe as those of the Spanish. It is the methods handed down by the Portuguese that I had the privilege of learning.

The art of reining the stock horse and the art of making the rawhide equipment and horsehair mecates have almost been lost. Most of the old-timers have died without passing on their knowledge, but some ranches in the Far West still practice and teach the art of reining, and some younger people have managed to find the means to learn to make the equipment.

Much of the onus for the loss of knowledge must be on horse shows. As less knowledgeable judges awarded the blues and purples to more spectacular but incorrect performances, trainers emulated those maneuvers and the rules changed to accommodate them. Today they even include a "turn on the center"—a thing no self-respecting reinsman would ever allow his horse to do.

Other "trainers" who wanted immediate results invented instruments of torture to replace the bosal. There were several forms of metal bosals that could do nothing but hurt the horse. The cable core bosal is an outgrowth of these inhumane tools. I hope what I have to say here will help you understand a little bit about the proper equipment and its use.

The selection of the hackamore is very important. It works on the horse's nose and under his jaw through pressure and immediate release. The bosal must have life to it, being neither raggy nor rigid. For this reason a bosal with a cable core is unacceptable as it takes force to spring its cheeks together. Also, most cable core bosals are made too long with too heavy a heel knot, making them hang improperly on the horse's nose.

A good bosal has a rawhide core, and you should be able to squeeze it closed with one hand about three inches from the heel knot. It should spring open when you release. You should be able to hold it by the heel knot and nosepiece and bend it back about thirty degrees and have it spring back when you release it.

Cheeks three-quarters of an inch in diameter make about the right weight of bosal for most of today's colts. The length, measured from the inside edge of the nosepiece to the inside base of the heel knot, should be eleven or twelve inches. If the bosal is too short, you can't take enough wraps with the mecate. If it is too long, it will need too many wraps and so be too heavy.

When the bosal is hung on the horse's head, the headstall string should lie just back of the horse's eyes. This gives the bosal the proper balance. While the nosepiece can have a little thickening in the center, it should not have a big lump. No thickening at all is better.

The bosal should be kept clean with glycerine saddle soap. Never use any sort of oil preparation on rawhide work because that will make it raggy. You should keep the nosepiece and cheeks of the bosal clean so the accumulated sweat, dirt, and hair don't sore the horse's nose and jaws.

The reason for using a mane hair mecate is that it has the right weight and is springy so the wraps do not pull down tight. This allows it to tighten the cheeks a little when you pull on the rein as in doubling and immediately release the cheeks when you release the pull. Good mecates are hard to find nowadays as most of them have quite a bit of tail hair in them. This isn't totally bad. It's just that they are more prickly with the stiff tail hairs sticking out, and they don't drape as nicely as the mane hair mecates.

No, the prickles do not help a horse learn to neck-rein better. He learns that through your proper use of the reins, your body, and your legs. It's just that the prickles are harder on your hands. One thing to watch out for in all mecates is that they are twisted evenly. If a strand is loose, either all the way or in spots, the rope can easily break.

We never tie up a horse with a mecate because it isn't strong enough if the horse pulls back on it. We initially use a tie rope and later on just take two or three wraps around the post or hitching rail with the mecate so it will slip loose if the horse suddenly pulls hard on it. This never worked with Dos Reales, though. He would always carefully test the rope by turning his head far enough to see if the rope would slip. If it did, then he calmly turned away and walked off. He was the only horse I ever had do this, but then he was very smart!

Because mecates are so hard to come by and are expensive, never drop the lead end on the ground where a horse can step on it and throw up his head and break it. The vaqueros never trained their horses to ground tie. They always taught them to stand "tied to the horn" for short periods and hobbled them for longer periods when having to dismount to work. Mecates can be cleaned by washing them in cool water and a mild detergent such as Woolite. Rinse them well and stretch them out straight to dry.

A mecate three-quarters to seven-eighths' inch diameter is the right size for training a horse. It wraps easily on the bosal and adds the right amount of weight. It should be 22 feet long to give you the right length of reins and lead rope. Today many trainers use a braided nylon rope the same size in place of the mecate. You must work a knot in one end of it so it won't pull through the bosal. I don't think there is really any substitute for the mecate but sometimes we must use the next best thing.

I have seen various instructions on wrapping the hackamore. One said to wet the bosal to soften it so you could set the nose part to be round and the cheeks near the heel knot to stay together. This is wrong because the cheeks on either side of the horse's jaw should spring closed and open—the basic principle of applying any rein aids.

A lot of the instruction on wrapping shows ways to wrap each cheek separately or says to pull the wraps tight. The wraps must go around both cheeks to spring them in and must be just snug, not tight, to allow them to spring out. I was taught by my vaquero mentor the very best way to wrap a hackamore.

While the length of the reins can vary some according to personal preference, they should be somewhere near fifty-six inches long for the average size horse with proportionate length neck. When the hackamore is on the horse, the reins should reach about the middle of the seat of the saddle. If they are too short, it hampers their use; too long makes them awkward to use and possibly dangerous. One old-timer remarked that he had seen the young riders using long hackamore reins so he decided to try it. His colt gave one buck jump and the reins flipped right over the old-timer's head. He immediately went back to the accustomed length!

To wrap the bosal, double the tassel end of the mecate so your reins are about fifty-six inches long. Bring the reins from the bottom of the bosal up between the cheeks and take one wrap around the left cheek toward the heel knot with the tassel end. With the long end of the mecate, take one wrap over the top of the cheeks from right to left in front of the reins. Take a second wrap in back of the reins and a half wrap to pull this end down between the cheeks from the top near the heel knot.

These wraps should be snugged down to lie flat against each other. The front wrap will be snug but not pulling the cheeks together. This is the basic number of wraps. If it is too many for proper adjustment on the colt, you need a longer bosal. If you must add more than two, you need a bosal that is an inch shorter. The adjustments are made with the hackamore on the horse.

In order to adjust the hackamore to the individual horse, you must

This is the best way to wrap a hackamore to make it the most effective. Snug the wraps down but don't pull them tight.

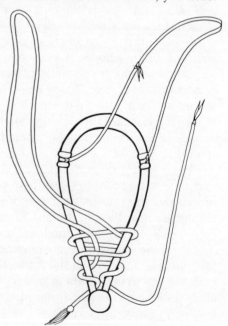

Starting the Colt

Pinch down the bridge of his nose to find the spot where he ducks his head slightly. The nosepiece goes on that spot.

have it on him in the proper place. To find this place, pinch on both sides of the broad bone down the front of his face. Start a little high and pinch, pinch, pinch downward until you reach the spot that makes him duck his head slightly. Adjust the headstall string so the nose-piece hangs on this spot. It is where the nerves are the most exposed, and the colt will feel the bosal and respond with the lightest use of the reins.

I have had some riders tell me that you must raise or lower the bosal a wee bit from time to time to keep the horse from getting heavy in the hackamore. I have ridden my horse for fourteen years with the adjustment the same and he has remained light. It is heavy hands that deaden the horse to the hackamore.

With the hackamore hung properly on the horse's nose, lift the heel knot with the reins. From hanging loose to contact with his jaw by the front wrap of the mecate, the distance traveled should be about an

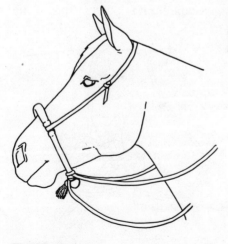

The exact placement of the hackamore varies with each horse, but it will be no higher than this.

The Hackamore   97

inch. Any less than this indicates the bosal is fitted too tight. Any more than this can rub the colt's jaw raw.

If the bosal with its two and a half wraps is too tight, get one that is a little bigger. If it is too loose, you can add the one or two wraps needed by loosening the wraps so you can work. Pull the lead end of the mecate out a ways to make it possible to add the one or two wraps needed below the wraps that are there. Pull the end of the mecate out of the added wraps and down between the cheeks and snug all of them down. You can subtract wraps the same way in reverse order.

There are several reasons for wrapping a hackamore this way. It is simple and easily adjusted. The reins are close to the horse's jaw to make the lifting action the most effective. The one wrap in front of the reins not only holds them in place but also forms a soft bar to contact the horse's jaw. The lead rope is at the back of the hackamore where it is best suited for leading the horse.

Some hackamores are fitted with a fiador (throatlatch). I have never cared for this because it changes the action of the hackamore somewhat and I didn't get such good results. Also, it is harder to put the wraps on and take them off because you must work in front of the fiador, not simply add or subtract over the end of the heel knot. The main purpose of a fiador is to keep the heel of the hackamore from pulling off the horse's chin if he jerks back when tied up or being led.

Without the fiador there is an easy way to overcome this problem. Take the off rein over the horse's poll short enough that it lifts the bosal tight against his jaw. Take the near rein up under his throat to be equal in holding up the bosal, and twist the two together twice close in his throat. Tie the doubled reins in two half hitches around both reins immediately below the twists. Pull the knots quite snug. The stretch of the knots and the mecate will take the pressure off his jaws and this "throatlatch" will keep the heel knot from slipping off the horse's chin if he should jerk back suddenly.

You can't hook the reins on the saddle horn to prevent this. If they

Tying the reins up for a throatlatch. Take the final half hitch with the doubled reins and pull the knot snug.

Starting the Colt

are hooked short enough to hold the heel knot on, you are pulling on the saddle horn instead of leading the colt. If they are loose enough for leading, they are ineffective. Until you are sure the colt will lead well, you should tie up the reins when leading any but a very short distance. Later on you needn't tie them up unless the situation calls for precautionary measures.

The vaqueros never used a halter on a hackamore horse. The colt was caught by roping and was snubbed to a post in the middle of the corral. From this he learned to respect a rope around his neck. Initially, a colt was tied up with a rope tied with a bowline snug in his throat and a bosal on his head. The bosal was hung high on the colt's nose; the tie rope was run between the cheeks of the bosal and tied around them with a half hitch in back of the rope to hold the heel knot up. From this education a colt learned to lead and tie up very well with just a rope around his neck tied snug in his throat with a bowline.

In more modern times more ranches halter-broke the colts at weaning time before turning them back out on the range. Halters came into more general use but the colts were still ridden with hackamores. For this reason the halters were always adjusted higher than usual for initial tying up and were even padded on the noseband with sheepskin if used on trained hackamore horses. This prevents the horses from becoming immune to the feel of the nosepiece and learning to lug on it. You should observe this practice with your hackamore horse when using a halter.

Because the action of the hackamore is different from that of the snaffle, there are some differences in the way you handle the reins. Initially, the colt responds to the pressure of the bosal on his nose. As he comes to an understanding of the action of the reins, he begins to respond to the feel of the bosal against his jaw as well.

While we never lift our hands more than a small amount with the snaffle, the action of the hackamore requires it to lift the heel of the bosal to contact the horse's jaw.

To the educated snaffle bit colt, contact is when the reins are almost taut, and he likes for this contact to be there at all times. The educated hackamore colt feels the contact when the reins are slightly loose and knows that it will get stronger as he feels the heel knot lifted off his chin. Unless the rider is quite insensitive, the horse is not so likely to be startled by much firmer contact because there is about an inch of travel that gradually makes the contact get firmer. The hackamore horse is ridden on a loose rein when just traveling from here to there. Both horses should be walked on a loose rein as a rest from concentrated work.

Because of the action of the hackamore, you must lift your hand by bending your elbow as you take on the rein. As the colt gets lighter in the hackamore, this lift will be sufficient with very little necessity to bring your hand back by swinging your arm at the shoulder. Because the hackamore reins come from almost the center of his jaw, you must continue to use a partial leading rein to turn him until he is totally obedient to neck-reining.

It is just as essential with the hackamore horse as with the snaffle bit horse that you use the reins with take and release and use your legs as you take on the reins. You always want to push the horse up to the bit or hackamore, never simply pull his head back. It is just as essential with both horses that you say "Please" by taking on the reins briefly as you squeeze with your legs to let him know you are going to ask something of him. And you say "Thank-you" with immediate release when he starts to do what you ask.

Both colts are educated with the leading rein that comes and goes. Beyond that the take and give with the snaffle is with fingers that close and relax on reins that are tightened more or less by swinging your arm back. The take and give with the hackamore reins is always an up-and-down motion over and over when asking anything of the colt. It is never a steadier strong pull with only flexible fingers. The exception in both cases is the initial pull in doubling, which is actually very brief. Of course, we never jerk on either the snaffle or the hackamore.

It is essential that all horses yield to the bit, and this is especially true of the hackamore horse. If he stiffens his neck and sticks his nose out, you have very little control of him. If he sticks his nose up in the air, you have no control at all. A horse should never be allowed to learn that what you put on his head can fail to control him.

You can't train a hackamore colt to yield to the bit by turning his head against the opposite fixed rein. You do it by keeping your hand low but not so low that it upsets your balance. With your hand about on the level of your seat and using a leading rein, you are applying stronger contact to his nose and the side of his jaw. There is almost no lift to the heel knot at this time. This action encourages him to tuck his nose down and back. You must move your hand smoothly out and in a short distance so there is give and take without any jerk. You don't use force to try to make him respond to the rein. You release the pull entirely when he turns his head.

You can start his education of yielding to the hackamore by standing beside him on each side to get him to turn his head. You can continue it when you are mounting him at his tying post, being sure he has enough slack in the tie rope to turn his head. During the first few rides you will continue to use this low leading rein and when he is responding well to it, you begin to raise your hand to lift the heel knot. Gradually the colt will respond because he sees your hand move out and feels the bosal lift against his jaw. Then you no longer need to carry your hand so low or use any noticeable pull to get him to turn except as a reminder when he is slow to respond.

Initially, you use two low leading hands to ask the colt to slow to the walk and stop. Here again, most of the action is on his nose, which encourages him to tuck and yield. Be sure to use your legs at the same time and to take and give on the reins. You must give him a soft warning with your hands and legs and then use them both over and over to get him to respond by tucking his nose and slowing and stopping.

Too often I see people who think they must jam a hackamore horse into the hackamore with a strong pull on the reins to ask for the stop. They know he is to learn to stop very quickly when asked and think he should be stopped that way from the beginning. The result is a horse that throws his head up and hops behind in a very rough stop.

First you must help him understand to stop with the two leading reins as I have described. Then you can gradually begin raising your hands to lift the heel knot. Gradually he will stop more readily, first from the walk, then from the trot, and later from the canter. This all builds up to his being responsive enough to stop readily from the gallop, balanced to the rear and with his nose tucked.

During all this training you must warn him with a lift of your hands and squeeze of your legs that you are going to ask for the halt. You must give him time to respond to the subsequent take and give of your hands and legs, and you must always apply the aids smoothly and carefully so he tucks his nose.

When he is fully trained, you still ask the same way by saying "Please" and following through with the take and give. That way he will perform willingly and correctly. You should not expect him to make a sliding stop except in slick footing. In all other footing, when coming to a quick full halt from a gallop the reined stock horse takes short walking steps behind.

Because of the sequence of educating the colt to respond to the hackamore, you initially ride with your hands lower and farther apart than with the snaffle. As he begins to get responsive to the lift of the reins, you can then carry your hands at about waist level, but they will still be farther apart than with the snaffle. Then most of the rein action will be by the lifting of your hands and a moderate leading rein. You still resort to the lower hand and more open leading rein as needed.

All of this talk about use of the reins is because it is easy to make a horse heavy in the hackamore if you are too heavy-handed. A colt does not become a hackamore horse simply because he wears the equipment. Putting a rein on him is an art that begins the moment you start riding him or even when you bit him in the corral. Because it is so difficult to describe feel in words, the best I can do is try to tell you the mechanics of it all.

The education of a hackamore colt in preparation for riding is quite similar to that of a snaffle bit colt. He should be tied up with either the halter or bosal as I described earlier in this chapter. He should be sacked out, saddled, and mounted the same way. He should be fitted with the hackamore and turned loose in the corral to get acquainted with it and the saddle. But he shouldn't be ground-driven because the weight and the action of the lines on the hackamore would make him less responsive to it when he is ridden.

In turning the colt loose saddled and bitted, tie the reins to the saddle horn so they don't lift the heel of the hackamore when his head is at rest but so they will tighten if he lowers his head more. *You do not set his head.* It will take him about three lessons to get acquainted with the feel of the hackamore and to give to it when it tightens.

At the end of the second bitting lesson you can start getting him to

"Bitted" with reins the right length so he lowers his head into the hackamore and yields to it. Never "bit" him tighter than this.

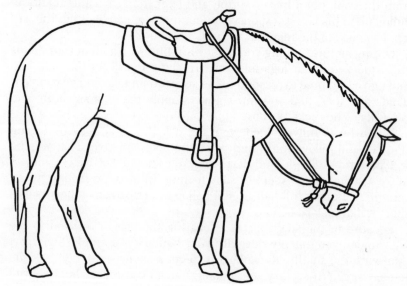

turn his head as you stand beside him. About the second time you mount him at his tying post after that, he should be accepting you well enough that you can turn his head then, too. When he is responding well to these exercises, it is time to ride him.

The first riding lesson is similar to the one for the snaffle bit colt. Get him walking forward well and making gradual turns and stops. As he shows understanding in the turning, make several turns toward the fence from about ten feet out to prepare him for his doubling lessons the next day.

All horsemen should keep in mind that a horse's obedience is largely mental. The equipment on his head gives you a means of communication. You can use the rein to bring his head to the side to get him to turn or both reins to bring his head back to get him to stop. If he doesn't respond, you haven't got through to his brain. It can be that he isn't very sensitive or that he has a basically selfish nature.

There are those who recommend bumping a colt's jaw with the bosal to make him respond, that is, using short, hard jerks. You should not do this with the hackamore any more than you should jerk on the snaffle. You need to be firmer with the less sensitive or more selfish colts, but you don't need to hurt them on the nose or in the mouth. Besides making them less trusting, to hurt them this way also makes them stick their noses up in the air, which is very bad training.

There is a simple way to help a colt understand to turn to the rein. When he is walking vigorously, his head nods up and down. Take minimum contact with the leading rein so it is very light when his head goes up. Hold your hand steady and he will nod his head into the rein, making the contact stronger. Keep him moving with your inside leg in small taps, and just hold the rein steady so he is taking and releasing as his head goes down and up. He will turn a little each time his head goes down. You can do this with either the snaffle or the hackamore.

If the colt just won't respond to turn, get off and remind him from the ground. If this doesn't work, tie up the reins to make the throatlatch and tie his head to his tail with the lead end of the mecate. Follow the instructions in chapter 10. *You must take him loose when he is turning.* Tying his head around once or twice usually gets him to understand he is to respond to the rein. It is not so severe with the hackamore as with the snaffle but still should be done only if necessary.

The second and third lessons in the round corral are the same as those for the snaffle bit colt. You continue to keep him moving forward well, give him practice in turning and stopping, and add trotting and doubling. In the arena you add the lope and doubling from it. You use the same exercises to improve his understanding and responses—circles, changes of gaits, turns, stopping, and standing. Be sure to use the leg aids the same as with the snaffle bit colt.

There are two more exercises you should start in the arena. When

Sometimes we must tie the hackamore colt's head to his tail. Always take him loose when he is turning to the pull. Never go off and leave him in this fix.

he is stopping readily from the walk, pause briefly and then ask him to walk on. This lays the foundation for his learning to jump out much later in his training. Don't expect him to respond quickly at first. Give him time to understand. By sometimes asking him to stand longer and sometimes asking him to pause and move on, you teach him to be alert for what you may ask of him.

The other exercise is the foundation for the turn on the haunches. This can begin as soon as he is starting to turn when seeing your hand out to the side and feeling the lift of the bosal against his jaw. Initially, all you ask for is a step to one side at a time in front with his hind feet in place. This evolves into a step to each side without moving his hind feet. With time and practice it eventually becomes the pickup or offset right and left.

Everything must be just right in order to get the step with the front feet. The colt must stop with all four feet under him, not sprawled out to the front. Unless he stops this way, don't attempt the turn on the

Doubling from the trot. At this point release the reins to let him finish the turn himself. It is a good training device for the hackamore horse, but don't overdo it.

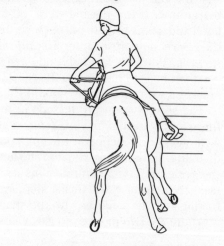

Starting the Colt

haunches. Later on after he has learned to back, you can ask him to lean back without stepping back and then ask for the step in front. For now he must be alert but relaxed and not trying to move on of his own accord.

You must be relaxed, too. If you stiffen your body, the colt won't respond because you won't automatically take the position for such a turn. You must use the leading rein with a little lift and must take on both reins just enough to prevent his taking a step forward. At the same time you must squeeze lightly with your legs in the position for an ordinary turn—outside leg back to hold his haunches in place.

You never kick or spur a horse on the outside shoulder to aid him in the turn on the haunches. This makes a hurried, lunging turn that gives you less control of his pickups. A stock horse should work precisely, not frantically. Besides, show rules forbid it and that's one show rule I agree with.

If you stay relaxed so you can feel all your aids and their effect on the colt and think of how the turn should feel as the colt does it, you will aid properly and get that one step to the side. That is theoretically true. Actually, it may take several tries before the colt understands what you are asking. Be patient. And when you get that step, don't get in a hurry to make it into several steps each way back and forth. Develop the turn on the haunches as the colt shows understanding and develops the ability—one step at a time.

A reined stock horse works on his haunches balanced to the rear with his hocks bent. His forehand will be raised. He doesn't work with his head down eye-to-eye with the cow the way a cutting horse does but picks up right and left when working in close. He stops square with his haunches lowered, his hocks bent, and his feet under his haunches, not on stiff hind legs shoved forward under his belly.

From the square stop he can pick up 180 degrees to turn back with

Taking the first step in the turn on the haunches. This is essential for the hackamore horse and a good exercise for the snaffle bit horse.

the cow and then pick up again to come on around if she escapes him. (It can happen to the best of them.) He is never asked for a rollback because he must often work in slippery footing. He is much less likely to fall if he stops square and then turns. He doesn't really lose any time in this maneuver.

From a stop or a pickup he can leap forward into an immediate halt or into a run. He must back readily, turn on the forehand, and side-pass. He must do all his work without getting excited and immediately stand or walk off quietly when asked. It takes about two years to finish this training and another six months to put him in the bridle. How well he accepts his training depends upon your patience and thoroughness in laying the foundation and developing his responses.

The vaqueros call this foundation training "putting the horse in the hackamore." Before he is considered in the hackamore, there are several things he must do readily. He must go forward freely in all gaits, relaxed and with long strides. He must yield to the hackamore with a little tuck of his nose each time you lift the reins. He should get so he yields to the lift going in all gaits, after each stop, and before and during each thing you ask him to do. He should stop readily from the walk, stand quietly, and readily move off in the walk from the halt.

When he does these well, he will walk out freely on a loose rein with his neck a little above level and his nose extended so he is carrying the hackamore. The vaqueros consider this a sign that he is truly in the hackamore.

From this you go on to teaching him to turn on his haunches, neck-rein, back, and gradually get more adept at the things you ask. When he is stopping readily from the walk and moving forward readily out of the halt, you can ask him to back the same way you would ask a snaffle bit colt.

Take on the reins just enough to restrain him from stepping forward

"In the hackamore." The horse's attitude and carriage show he has accepted it.

and squeeze with your legs. Release the aids as he does. As soon as he understands this to step back, just lift the reins at the same time you squeeze with your legs. Coordinate it so he does step back, and repeat it for each step he is to take. While he should stand quietly after backing, he should also be moved forward in the walk to prepare him for learning to jump ahead later on.

When he is beginning to respond to the lift of the reins so you are carrying your hands higher, you should move both hands in turning him. They stay about the same distance apart, and the outside hand comes a little across his withers while the inside hand turns him with the amount of leading rein needed. Gradually less leading rein is needed, so your hands stay about the same distance apart in turning as in going straight.

In moving both hands in turning you are teaching the horse to neck-rein. Neck-reining is never done with force. The only time it is done up in the middle of the horse's neck is during roping, when the coils of the rope must be kept out of the way of taking your dallies on the saddle horn.

In neck-reining, the horse is responding to your leg aids and the position of your body as well as the touch of the rein on his neck. He learns to respond to the touch on his neck because it is there when you move both hands over to turn him with the inside hand. Any time any horse doesn't want to obey the neck rein, help him understand that he must by using the inside leading rein, not by using more force with the neck-reining.

The hackamore is ideal for teaching neck-reining because the pull on the left rein brings the right cheek of the bosal into contact. With

After the colt knows to turn, you use both hands in unison and he just naturally learns to neck-rein.

the hackamore you don't even need to think about this part of his training if you always move both hands over, use your legs consistently, and look where you want to go so your body will position itself properly. You'll just discover one day that your colt has learned to respond to the touch of that rein.

I see today's riders bridging the reins, and that is helpful to bring the outside hand over with the turning hand. Bridging the reins is simply taking the right rein in the left hand along with the left rein and the left rein in the right hand along with the right rein. With the reins taut between your hands there should be about ten inches between them. I don't care to bridge the reins myself because I want more independence with my hands so I can use more leading rein when needed. If you bridge the reins, let them slip through your hands when you need more leading rein. You don't want to exert more pressure on the outside rein at that time.

Most of your work should be done out on the trail. There the colt will be more willing to move out enthusiastically because it is more interesting to him. You will find places where you can gallop him up long grades or in circles on the flat. Just climbing up and down hills in the walk will help his balance to the rear.

You will find brush handy to work him back and forth against to improve his turns on the haunches. You can help him start learning about the pickup by asking for such turns over the end of a log. You can find places such as cut banks or high brush to double him against,

The two tufts of mane in the saddle roach indicate that the horse is in the two-rein. One tuft means he is straight up in the bridle. A smooth roach warns the vaquero to ride him only in the hackamore.

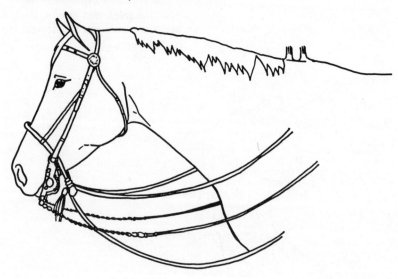

Starting the Colt

since doubling a hackamore colt is part of his training to get him balanced toward the rear. Just don't overdo it.

By putting in all his basic maneuvers now and then at places that seem to give him a reason, you will be more relaxed in the teaching and he will learn more readily. Don't try to hurry his education because that is a good way to spoil what he has already learned. Everyone should feel his way through training—feel how he is asking, feel if the horse is ready, and feel his response.

An early-day ranch custom is interesting. All cowboys pull the saddle horses' tails to hock length to keep them from catching on the brush. On ranches where the hackamore and spade bit were used, it was a sign that the colt had been ridden at least once or twice. It was considered foul play to pull his tail before he was ridden.

After his first ride, the colt's mane was roached the first six or seven inches at the withers. When he advanced to the two-rein, two tufts of hair about an inch wide and high were left standing in this roach and only one tuft when he was straight up in the bridle. These markings told any vaquero what to use on the horse's head. It was more than a misdemeanor to use a bridle on a hackamore colt.

15
Hobbling, Sidelining, and Staking

I have put this chapter last because I don't want you to feel it is something that you must do. Only those who are experienced in handling ropes in connection with horses and doing it in a way to avoid fighting with them should try sidelining a colt. Training a colt to stand hobbled isn't quite so difficult, but it can be somewhat alarming to a person who hasn't seen it done enough times to realize that the colt won't hurt himself.

When I have a good round corral to work in, I hobble and sideline a colt to sack him out, saddle him, and mount him. It is when I don't have such a corral that I tie a colt up for these things. Tying is just as effective in controlling him, but there are certain added benefits that accompany hobbling and sidelining.

For one thing, it is easier to groom and saddle a hobbled horse as there is no tie rope to duck under. A horse that is trained to stand hobbled can be safely restrained this way when there is no safe place to tie him.

Years ago I went on a group trail ride that took us into a secluded canyon where we ate lunch and participated in a play-day horse show before riding back out. The organizers had stretched out a long wire cable for a picket line. As my friends and I were approaching the picket line to tie our horses, one that was already tied there spooked and ran right down the cable into horses tied on either side of it. The cable was smoother than a regular picket rope and let the tie rope slide as if greased.

My friends and I decided tying there wasn't such a good idea. I think they found suitable trees for tying but may have had to hold their horses. I simply hobbled mine on the fringe of the activity where I could keep an eye on him. He was one that would have stood hobbled in the middle of downtown Los Angeles. Not all hobble-trained horses stand that well.

Both hobbling and sidelining help teach a horse not to fight if he gets his feet tangled in wire or brush. Sidelining also helps him learn to let you hold up his hind feet for cleaning, trimming, and shoeing if he hasn't benefited from that education early in his life. Even if I'm starting a gentle colt, I hobble and sideline him because of these educational advantages.

Iam was a gentle, friendly colt and when I sidelined him, his body and facial expressions soon became those of, "Why are you treating me this way?" Seeing this, I hugged his head and told him I still loved him. He immediately perked up, his eyes brightened, and he finished his sidelining lessons without any further self-pity.

Once when I was riding Frosty down a slope strewn with rocks and dead brush, I felt her make a short stride behind. I immediately stopped her and leaned over to see what the trouble might be. She had stepped into the fork of a Y-shaped, six-foot dead manzanita branch. Her hind pastern was wedged into the Y and when she tried to step, she lifted the whole thing. I dismounted, removed the manzanita, and said a prayer of thanks that I had sidelined her. If she had panicked, she could have run the end of that branch right into her belly—not to mention dumping me on the rocks.

Another incident had somewhat negative results. My daughter's Arabian filly, Shemali, was staying at our place in the foothills and Swede, Shemali's purebred "uncle," was there for me to start under saddle. Generally speaking, Arabians have more curiosity than some other breeds so Shemali led the small band of horses on an exploring trip. Farther from home they ran into some remnants of a barbed wire fence left over from an abandoned homestead. Both Shemali and Swede, who were no doubt in the lead, were cut on the wire—thankfully not seriously.

Because Swede hadn't been with me more than a week, his lessons hadn't begun and he hadn't been sidelined. He had been so scared by the incident that no matter what I tried, I never could get him over his fear of the zing of a moving wire. He did learn one handy thing from it, though. He could spot a wire fence even if it was rusty and hidden in the brush and grass, and so avoid stepping on it.

Besides teaching most horses not to fight when their feet get tangled in wire or brush, sidelining helps instill in them respect for the handler. They understand that you are the one who tied them up but then they learn for themselves that it is useless to struggle. Thus they not only respect the ties that bind but also respect your authority over them without your ever jerking them around in any way.

Sidelining also makes your work easier after the initial labor of getting that foot up. You can work all around the colt in sacking out, eventually even shaking out the sack in front of him—a thing you don't want to do to a colt that is tied up. You can crawl all over his back and even slide off his rump safely to get him used to whatever movements you might make in riding him. You must be more careful, however, in mounting him saddled as you could get caught if he spooks enough to throw himself down. For that reason I keep my feet out of the stirrups when in the saddle so I can push myself clear if need be.

Sidelining is also very useful in curing a colt of wanting to kick. Ilak was a very gentle filly, but for some unknown reason she decided to start kicking at me regularly. I sidelined her and stood in back of the foot that was taken up just off the ground. Making sure I was out of reach, I pulled her tail to shorten and shape it. It irritated her just enough to make her try to kick and learn that it was useless since it only jerked her neck and foot. I did this ten minutes each day for four days straight alternating sides. She never offered to kick again.

While there are these advantages, it would not work in your favor to try to sideline a colt if you aren't practiced in handling ropes around horses. You don't have to be so experienced to train a colt to hobble.

In the round corral—or any corral of similar size with fairly soft footing and no rocks—training a colt to hobble is rather simple. You need a gunnysack or soft five-eighths'-inch cotton rope to start and saddle hobbles to finish. In the first hobbling lesson the hobbles usually slip down around the colt's pasterns during his struggles. Leather hobbles or hard twist rope can burn him at that time. If using the gunnysack, open it up into a flat piece, fold it diagonally, and roll and twist it into a rope. The cotton rope should be at least five feet long.

For the first lesson take along an extra gunnysack or a pair of old blue jeans, a saddle blanket, and a rope for sacking out. Carry a sharp knife in your pocket as you may need it to cut the hobbles off at the end of the lesson. The knot can get pulled too tight to let you untie it easily.

Lead the colt into the middle of the corral and toss the end of the lead rope out in front of him so there are no kinks or coils to put your foot in. You can loosely hold the lead rope in your hand or let it drape across your arm as you work—just don't wrap it around your arm. Start by rubbing the sack hobbles up and down his front legs and holding it around his off cannon and give little tugs on it. You want him to understand that you are going to manipulate this sack around his front legs and that you want him to stand still while you do, so don't be so sudden that you excite him into moving. Coax him to stand.

When he accepts the feel and pull of the sack on his front legs, get him to stand with them quite close together. Often you must pick up one foot to set it down closer and repeat until he leaves it there. Now take the middle of the sack hobbles around the outside of his off cannon, and twist the two sides together snugly against it, with two or three more twists than it takes to reach the inside of his near cannon.

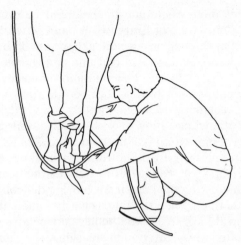

Putting on the sack hobbles. Take more twists than needed between his legs and tie the ends around the near cannon with a square knot. The lead rope draped over your arm this way is within reach if needed and is safe.

Take each end of the hobbles around the near cannon and tie them snugly with a square knot. You need those extra twists so the stretch of the sack or soft rope won't loosen the hobbles enough to let the colt pull a foot out of them.

Do this work slowly enough that the colt doesn't move until the knot is firmly tied. It isn't too difficult to get him to stand if you carry on a conversation with him and avoid sudden jerks on the hobbles. You want to avoid his getting the idea that he can break out of the hobbles.

When he is securely hobbled, drop the lead rope and step back out of the way. You can expect him to try to take a step and put his foot back down or take one or more tripping steps and fall to his knees or lunge into one or more galloping leaps. I just stay out of the way and let him figure it out for himself unless he makes more than three consecutive leaps. In that case I throw the saddle blanket out in front of him to stop him. I don't want him to get adept at traveling in the hobbles.

With the galloper I get up to him and hold the lead rope so I can discourage him with tugs on it from taking off again. To do this safely you must understand that the tug can turn his head toward you, so he may lunge in your direction. He isn't trying to leap on you, but you must step out of the way to avoid his accidentally doing so. If you train a colt to hobble out in the open, you must hold onto the lead rope to keep him under moderate control, and staying out of his way applies there too.

When the colt decides that it is better to stand in the hobbles, I sack him out as I described in chapter 7, holding the lead rope loosely if I have to work out in the open. The principle is the same—to get him used to the sack or blue jeans, the saddle blanket, and the rope so he knows they won't hurt him.

In this case there is one exception. If the colt doesn't try at all to

Hobbling, Sidelining, and Staking

move a front foot, I get a little more vigorous with the initial sacking out to see if he will try—but only try, not lunge off in panic. I want him to know he is restrained at the beginning rather than find it out later under less-controlled circumstances. I've had one or two colts that refused to try the hobbles even when sacked out more vigorously. Those colts never gave any subsequent trouble, but you do want to find out early what the colt's reaction is to the hobbles.

As you can surmise, I do the whole series of sacking out the first day of hobbling. It doesn't take more than half an hour to go through the repertoire. At the end of the lesson, I rub the colt's legs and tug a little on the hobbles to see that he will stand. Then I work carefully to keep him standing while I am untying the knot and removing the hobbles so he doesn't break out of them when the knot is partly untied. If he has struggled a lot, you will have to cut the hobbles off near the knot. To lead him away you often must turn him to one side to get him to take a step. It's amusing to see him move a leg forward carefully to be sure it is free.

If you just want your colt to learn to stand hobbled for convenience's sake, you can do it during the time you are sacking him out or wait until after ground driving or even his first rides. Even if you do it later than in his initial training, do sack him out in his first three hobbling lessons. Three lessons are usually enough to train a horse to hobble if you continue to hobble him fairly often to keep him in practice.

After the first lesson you can use the regular saddle hobbles around his cannons. I carry them on my saddle to have available when needed. If you are caught out without them and need to hobble your horse, you can use the end of your lead rope. Tie it on his cannons the way you did in his first lesson. Never use saddle hobbles as grazing hobbles because it will teach him to travel in them. Use regular grazing hobbles on his pasterns.

For the second lesson in starting a colt, I take the sacking out equipment, hobbles, saddle, saddle blankets, and bridle or hackamore into the corral. The equipment needed for sidelining is a three-quarter-inch

Two types of saddle hobbles. Don't use them for grazing as the horse will learn to travel in them.

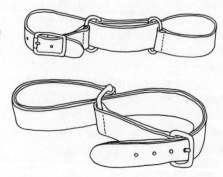

Starting the Colt

cotton rope thirty feet long and a foot strap. This is a soft leather strap one and a half inches wide, doubled and securely fastened into a three-inch harness ring at each end. The overall length including the rings is about twelve inches.

With all this equipment in the corral, I lead the colt in and hobble him in the middle of the corral to give him a refresher in sacking out, which reminds him to stand. I then tie the sideline with a bowline very snug around his neck just in front of his withers. The rope will stretch some when the colt struggles against it, and I don't want a big loop for him to get caught in.

Next I thread the end of the rope through both rings of the foot strap so it forms a U and then take the end of the rope over the top of the neck rope close to the bowline and under the neck rope from front to back. This is very important. If you simply bring it under the neck rope from back to front, you have no leverage to hold it when taking up the foot. With it threaded from front to back you can step toward the colt's head and have a dally on the neck rope to prevent his jerking his foot down before you can tie the rope.

So I now have the rope threaded through the foot strap and through the neck rope leaving enough slack that I can get the strap on his foot. I toss the foot strap under his belly to the opposite side. When the bowline is on the near side, I take up the off hind foot and vice versa. This is an important safety measure because a horse usually goes down in his struggles and can stifle himself if you take up the foot on the same side as the bowline. Taking up the opposite foot pulls it under his belly where it naturally belongs, instead of out to the side.

Because this is a gentle colt that I'm working with, I simply open up the foot strap, lift his foot, and put the strap around the back of his pastern and the rope in front. Then I go back to the near side, take up the slack in the rope without putting any pressure on his foot, and remove the hobbles. Now I gradually take up more and more on the

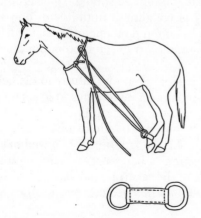

This shows the sideline and foot strap in place and the foot strap detail. Gradually take up the foot until it is halfway to his belly. Tie it up with two half hitches, with the loop of the rope around the two ropes just below the neck rope.

Hobbling, Sidelining, and Staking

rope until I have his foot halfway up to his belly. Then I tie two half hitches around both parts of the rope just below the bowline knot.

I tie these half hitches on the bight of the rope, not by pulling the end through because that would take too long to get it tied. If the colt struggles before I can start the knot, I step to the front to hold the rope from slipping. When he stops struggling, I continue until I succeed in getting his foot securely tied up. Then I step back and let him learn for himself that it is useless to struggle when a foot is caught.

I don't just move in and try to get that foot up as fast as possible. I take it by degrees so the colt has a chance to see what is happening and how each little bit feels. It's those who want to play cowboy and see how fast they can tie him up like a Christmas package who provoke a colt into rebellion. My aim is to educate, not aggravate.

The reason for using a foot strap instead of just taking the rope around the back of the pastern is to avoid rope burn. Also, the colt can get his foot out of the rope if it is just looped around it. The vaqueros used the foot strap and could put it on a wild colt with lots of patience and what appears to be sleight of hand.

The rope is threaded through one ring of the strap from outside to inside and the end of the rope is tied to the neck rope. (The colt is tied up for this operation.) The foot strap at the looped end of the rope is tossed between the colt's hind legs and pulled within safe reach with a baling wire hook. This can take several tries before the colt will stand still for it. The doubled rope is then brought around the outside of the off leg above the hock, and the strap end is tossed under the colt's belly to the near side.

Going back to the near side, the vaquero unties the end of the rope, maintains just enough tension to keep it around the off leg above the hock, and threads the end through the other ring of the foot strap from inside to outside. Now all he must do is pull the end of the rope while maintaining this tension. When he gets it all pulled through the rings, the strap slips around to the back of the colt's leg and the rope is across the front. It is then just a matter of wiggling it until it slips down to the pastern. It is quite a neat trick. I often do it on gentle colts just to keep in practice, even though I wouldn't try it on a bronc for fear of getting my head kicked off.

To get back to this colt with his foot taken up halfway to his belly. By now he may have thrown himself one or more times. It looks rough but is a lot better for him than his doing it when caught in wire. When he decides to stand quietly, I sack him out as the day before. In my younger days I then crawled up on his back, but now I do well to hop up and down beside him. This mounting bareback and later with the saddle should be done on the side of the taken-up foot to avoid getting caught in the sideline. I never mount a hobbled colt because he can't catch his balance.

The saddling comes next and is done the same way as I described, cinching up smoothly and tugging on it before taking it tighter. Then I bridle the colt or fit the hackamore to his head as the case may be, let his foot down, remove the rope, and turn him loose properly bitted.

The third day is a repetition of the second day, except I tie the bowline on the off side and take up the near hind foot. After saddling him, I may mount him but am prepared to thrust myself out of the saddle if he starts to struggle too much. Then I mount him again.

The fourth and fifth days I again sideline the colt once on each side to reinforce his education about things that tangle his feet. The only difference is that I don't take his foot up quite so high—only about eight inches off the ground. I sack him out, saddle him, mount him, and then bit him to turn him loose. From then on I hobble him for saddling and unsaddling. I usually ride a colt after the sixth or seventh day, but you can go on to ground driving and the training I have described.

Colts respond in different ways to sidelining. Some fight it more than others, throwing themselves several times before realizing it is better to stand. Then there was Coltburger. He looked the situation over, thought about it for a minute or two, and then heaved himself forward and down. Then he just lay there. I took the foot strap off and encouraged him to get up. Nothing doing. I finally had to remove the rope from his neck, too, and coax some more before he would get to his feet. He didn't act especially scared—more as if to say, "If this is where you want me, this is where I'll stay."

Before taking the foot loose, I lift it with the rope and then lift the foot itself, each time holding it briefly until the colt no longer tries to take it away. This helps the colt that hasn't had his feet picked up to learn that it is okay. If you are starting a mustang, it is the best way because he can't get completely loose if he jerks his foot away from you. That way he learns to accept having his feet picked up without presenting a danger to you.

There is another thing that is handy for a horse to know, especially if you plan to take him on camping trips. This is staking out. The vaqueros did it routinely because the wrangler's horse and the horses of the night riders had to be ready for use, whereas the rest of the caballada was turned loose to graze until needed.

You can't just take a horse out and tie him to a stake and expect him to stay out of trouble. Ninety-nine times out of a hundred he will wrap the stake rope around a hind pastern and burn himself. The vaqueros made a special stake rope to help avoid this problem.

They used the hide from a winter-butchered steer so the hair would be thick. After cutting off the legs and neck of the hide, they cut it in a one-inch strip by starting at the outside edge and going around and around until reaching almost the center of the hide. This long strip was soaked in water to make it pliable and then doubled in the middle through a large harness ring.

The vaqueros then jacked up the wheel of a wagon, fastened the harness ring to the hub, and twisted the two strands together hair side out by turning the wheel. When the rope was twisted snug full length, they lowered the wagon wheel and pegged down the other end of the rope so it was stretched taut to dry. This stake rope was stiff enough that it wouldn't tighten around the horse's pastern, thus making it easier for him to step out of it. The hair acted as padding to help avoid rope burns.

A good substitute for this rawhide stake rope is a thirty-foot, half-inch nylon rope run through a fourteen-foot length of garden hose. To make knot tying easier, an old, raggy lass rope will work or use a softer nylon rope. With the hose on the rope, tie a single knot seven feet from the end that will go around the horse's neck, push the hose against it, and tie another single knot at the other end of the hose. This will keep the hose in place.

The horse should be staked in an open area that is free of rocks and brush and other obstacles. This is true even for the trained stake horse, since getting the rope tangled around such things can cause the horse to get tangled in the rope. For the training the ground should be soft just in case he does fall down.

When training, the best thing to tie the stake rope to is a heavy iron implement wheel such as was on a horse-drawn mowing machine. Such a wheel is heavy enough that the horse can't run off with it, but it is also movable enough that it will give some under strain, thus lessening the pull on the horse's head. You tie the stake rope to the rim of such a wheel and it will turn as the horse goes around it and will dig into the ground some if he pulls straight away.

I realize that finding this sort of wheel could be difficult, but knowing the desired functions of it could help you find a substitute, such as a wheel from an eighteen-wheeler. A log is a good thing to tie to if it is about twenty feet long and over twelve inches in diameter in the middle. If you don't have any of these available, it is better to tie to something solid, such as the base of a tree or solid post, than to tie to anything the colt can pull up or drag off.

To stake out the colt use a strong nylon halter. If you plan to ride him in the hackamore, adjust it so the noseband is higher than where the bosal will be hung on his nose. This will keep him from becoming deadened to the feel there. Run the end of the stake rope through the halter ring and tie it with a bowline quite snug at his throat when his head is at rest.

If you must tie the other end of the stake rope to something quite large, such as the base of a large tree, use another strong rope around it and tie the stake rope to that rope. Otherwise, tie it to the wheel rim or the center of the heavy log by taking two wraps around and then tying a slipknot. Make sure all knots are snugged down so they won't work loose.

It is best to do the stake training after the colt has been sacked out thoroughly—even better if he has been hobbled and sidelined as well. These get him used to rope and other things around him so he won't have so many new things to contend with when he is staked.

Have everything ready at the staking place. Halter the colt, run the end of the stake rope through the halter ring, and tie it on his neck. Let the rope drag beside him as you lead him out. This will alert him to be aware of the rope on the ground. If he wants to spook at it dragging, stop briefly to let him catch his breath and then lead him on. Keep him under control with the stake rope draped over your arm while you secure the other end to the anchor. Then step back and let him figure it out.

I don't believe in going away and leaving the colt to fate. You could come back to find him wrapped up like a spool of thread. I keep watch from a distance because he can get in a bind where he needs help even with the hose on the rope. When the rope is wrapped around a hind pastern and the colt is facing the anchor, the more he tightens the rope the more it pulls on his head, making him back up and tighten it more.

If after a few minutes he just can't figure out how to get out of this mess, I help him out by snapping a lead rope on the halter and turning him away from the stake rope as I lead him forward. Then I remove the lead rope and again let him do his own thing.

Even when the horse is well trained to stake, I would usually use the stake rope with the hose on it as a precaution. That depends upon how smart the horse has become in watching the rope. Some horses are a whole lot better at this than others and can be staked with any

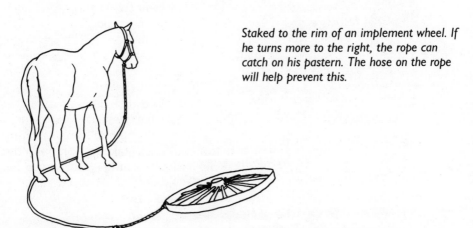

Staked to the rim of an implement wheel. If he turns more to the right, the rope can catch on his pastern. The hose on the rope will help prevent this.

Hobbling, Sidelining, and Staking

strong thirty-foot rope to anything solid enough to hold them. No matter how watchful he is, he can't figure out how to avoid tangling the rope on obstacles, so again I must warn you to stake him in an open area always.

Because there is always a chance of an accident where horses are concerned, never stake him to anything he can break, pull out of the ground, or run off with. Personally, I don't care for picket pins because they can be pulled out of the ground and the horse can roll on them and injure himself. The kind that screw into the ground and have a rounded loop on top may be okay—I've never used one. A fifteen-inch length of reinforcing rod with a rounded knob welded on top would make a good picket pin. It should be driven deep into the ground to keep it in place. The knob should be big enough to keep the rope from slipping off. You might even consider painting the knob bright yellow so it will stand out as something different to him—unless you stake him in a host of golden daffodils.

If you are training your horse to stake so you can take him camping or some such trip, do the training several weeks before. After he is trained, continue to stake him at least once or twice a week to keep him in practice. You must reinforce his training with repetition so staking is firmly implanted in his memory bank. It is also wise to stake him several times before the next trip if some time has passed without staking him.

I said it in the beginning of this chapter and I must repeat it here. Don't try these things unless you are handy with ropes and know how to use them safely around horses and yourself. Keep in mind that these things are educational for the horse—not a means of exerting your brutal authority over him. They are ways of putting a horse under control in such a way that he can learn for himself how to handle difficult situations that could endanger both you and him.

Afterthought

In looking back over what I have written, I find it gives the impression of western motif. This shouldn't surprise me since my childhood dream was to go West and be a cowboy. What does surprise me is how often I must repeat that there is no basic difference between western and English riding when they are done according to the horse.

I recently was giving some lessons to a girl using my horse and stock saddle. Her seat was rather bouncy so I was teaching her to post. I explained to her that cowboys do post the trot, and the object of posting is to save the horse's back as well as the rider's bottom.

At the next lesson she asked me, "Should I buy an English saddle when I get my horse?"

"Why would you do that when you are having difficulty staying on the western saddle?" I asked.

Her reply was typical of what I hear from people of all degrees of expertise. "I thought I should get an English saddle because you are teaching me to post and that is English riding."

While it is true that there are various styles of riding, they are just that—the way of riding that is fashionable at the moment for any one breed, show class, equine sport, or just pleasure riding. These are styles that change with the times and, sadly, many of them have nothing to do with horsemanship.

In all of my teachings I stick to one principle without digression. Every equine is an equine regardless of his outward appearance or breeding. In watching a program on zebras, I had snorted to myself when they said the observations of zebra behavior were from a study made possible by a large grant of money. There wasn't one bit of zebra behavior reported in that program that couldn't have been learned from watching a band of breeding horses running on the range.

"And God made the beast of the earth after its kind, and cattle after their kind, and every thing that creepeth upon the earth after its kind: and God saw that it was good."—Genesis 1 : 25

So please remember—no matter what style you prefer, the things I teach have their foundation in the physical, mental, and psychological makeup of the horse no matter what his habitat or his markings.

Index